BLUE

All Rise

Our Story

ONE PLACE. MANY STORIES

HQ
An imprint of HarperCollins*Publishers* Ltd
1 London Bridge Street
London SE1 9GF

This hardback edition 2017

1
First published in Great Britain by
HQ, an imprint of HarperCollins*Publishers* Ltd 2017

A catalogue record for this book is
available from the British Library.

ISBN: 9780008222208

Typeset in Bembo Std 11.75/16 pt by
Palimpsest Book Production Limited, Falkirk, Stirlingshire

Printed and bound in Great Britain by
CPI Group (UK) Ltd, Croydon, CR0 4YY

MIX
Paper from
responsible sources
FSC **FSC™ C007454**
www.fsc.org

This book is produced from independently certified FSC™ paper
to ensure responsible forest management.

For more information visit: www.harpercollins.co.uk/green

For the fans

CONTENTS

'ONE LOVE'

20 February 2002 – Brit Awards, Earl's Court, London

ANTONY

This was meant to be one of the best nights of Frank Skinner's career, and just another evening out for the four of us. But the Fates, it seems, have other plans.

I've always loved Frank, and he's definitely looking the part for one of the biggest jobs of his life – hosting the music industry's most important event of the year, broadcasting live to millions of viewers at home, as well as entertaining us lot sitting in front of him. He bounds onto the stage at the start, smiling like the cat that got the cream, ready with a good joke to share. Sure enough, when he undoes his jacket, there it is – a big shiny Union Jack tie and shirt underneath. Not quite as stunning as Geri Halliwell in THAT dress, but still, pretty funny.

Sadly for Frank, it turns out that is to be his best moment, and we watch him bumble his way through the next two hours. His one-liners are falling on stony ground, while his co-host, Zoe Ball, stands beside him, looking increasingly unhappy. Frank will say later he was dying inside, this was the worst gig he's ever done, one he will never, ever repeat — which is a shame as, only a few yards away at one of the tables, the four of us are having a whale of a time.

DUNCAN

This is actually one of Blue's first proper grown-up nights out. The band's only been together for a few months, and most of our evenings tend to end up in clubs where . . . well, let's just say the wine might not be as good as at the Brits and the floor's definitely a lot dirtier. And the places we hang out, you certainly don't get to see Anastasia duetting with Jamiroquai, the first act on tonight's bill. We all grew up watching these awards on TV, so when our record label told us we'd been nominated for the Breakthrough gong, there was only a pile of dust where we'd been standing; we'd already gone to pick out our suits.

LEE

The two best things about tonight — wearing a great suit, and the fact that we already know we're not going to win. I'm not being falsely modest here, check out this list of our fellow nominees . . . our great mates Atomic Kitten, Starsailor, Mis-Teeq, So Solid Crew, Turin Brakes, Tom McRae, Zero 7, Elbow. Not enough talent on that list for you? Oh sorry, I forgot to mention Gorillaz in there as well. See what I mean?

So we're not feeling any pressure, the wine's flowing and we can revel in sitting in our glad rags at one of the top tables, gazing at proper stars like Kylie Minogue and Sting, laughing with — mostly *at* — Frank Skinner, and generally pinching ourselves.

'ONE LOVE'

SIMON

You know what, Frank's actually pretty funny up there – but the four of us have always been easy to please. So we're giggling our way through the night, while our glasses continue to be filled by an invisible hand. In fact, we're having such a good time we almost miss our category being announced, until Trevor Nelson comes on stage to present the award: he looks the business.

ANTONY

Suddenly everything slows, and it feels like someone has turned the volume right down in this giant arena. Trevor slowly opens the envelope, and, is it me, or has the whole room gone completely still? It feels like five minutes, but it's probably only a couple of seconds before he says one word, 'Blue.'

DUNCAN

Now it's a blur of hugs, the four of us jumping up and down, somehow making it onto the stage, gazing out at a sea of faces. I'm completely tongue-tied, but I'm in front of the microphone, so I mumble something about thanking the record label. Then Antony takes a turn, and he thanks the fans – I wish I'd done that first. Somehow, he always finds it easier to come up with the patter.

LEE

I'm gazing at the Award in front of us, and I'm remembering those days at school, when a teacher told me, 'You'll never make it as a singer.'

Then I start jumping up and down in the background – there's always one!

SIMON

Cameras are flashing from every direction as we head backstage to more hugs. Everyone looks genuinely happy for us. It's a myth that nobody gets on in the music industry. There are some great people if you know where to look, and we've been lucky.

DUNCAN

The Westlife boys are the first to come up to us, which means a lot. And then, wow . . . I'm dreaming! It's Kylie, the princess I had on my wall back in Devon when I started dreaming about all of this. I can't wait to tell my mum.

LEE

I'm laughing because Antony's looking at the award in his hand and I've spotted him tearing up – he thinks no one's noticed.

ANTONY

Lee gets a bit weepy, which is fair enough – he's the youngest.

SIMON

I'm thinking, is this really happening? We're just four silly lads in borrowed suits.

'ONE LOVE'

ANTONY

Half an hour later and we're making our way into the after-show party in Knightsbridge. It's only 11 miles from where I grew up in Edgware, but we could be on a different planet. The club's party planners have gone overboard, and we walk along a stunning glass bridge, decked out with candles and coloured lights. More cameras flash as we get to the door – there are people everywhere. I can see my mum standing next to Duncan's – two familiar faces at the centre of all this alien glamour, bizarrely the most surreal sight of all.

DUNCAN

I go straight over to see them. I've already phoned my mum from the car, but seeing her is what brings home just how special this all is. She whispers in my ear about how proud my grandparents would be. We lost them both within the last two years, and I give her another hug. But this isn't a night to be sad.

LEE

I have to say, considering what a brain-ache we've been for our management on occasion, they know how to put on a party for us. They've been very generous tonight; the champagne is on tap, and I mean that literally, there it is in the middle of the bar. The music's loud, and everyone in the room wants to congratulate us, praise us, take our photo, introduce us to someone else. Those other, cooler boys in school we always wanted to be? That's us. Will I remember any of this in 16 years time? Possibly not. How can my ego withstand all this? I'll worry about that tomorrow.

SIMON

The night goes on, and some time later, I spot my brother Duane over by the bar. He's standing by himself, looking neither elated, nor jaded, by all this euphoric frenzy around him. Instead he looks bemused. I head over to him and for a few moments, neither of us says anything. Instead I join him in contemplating the scene, as if from outside looking in.

There's Antony, the one I met last but now spend the most time with. He's usually the most wary one in the band, the one reminding the rest of us not to count our chickens, that we have to read the small print – 'Baby steps, people' – but tonight he's as happy as the rest of us, standing in the middle of his huge family, making them laugh with his impressions.

Duncan's with his mum. It's always been just the pair of them, and I've never seen a mother and son as close as those two. Tonight will mean as much to her as it does to him.

Lee's laughing, dancing, surrounded by ladies, giving each of them his attention in turn. He doesn't have a worry in the world, that one, and as another stunning girl goes up to give him a congratulatory hug, he looks over her shoulder and tips me a huge, happy wink.

So why do I say what I say next to my brother? Is it the rollercoaster ride we've already been on, the one quick year that's seen us top the charts with our very first efforts, but also seen us come under attack, with astonishing abuse and even death threats? Or is it witnessing someone as armour-plated as Frank Skinner come unstuck when he least expected it earlier tonight? Is it the dark angel that sits quietly on my shoulder, and whispers tirelessly in my ear, as she always has since my childhood? Or is the overwhelming glamour of this night the proof I need that we are four very ordinary lads living an extraordinary existence for which we might not always be equipped? Tonight's seen us join a brand new club, membership elite. Is it my imagination, or is life about to get a lot more complicated?

I should add I've also drunk rather a lot of the fine champagne on offer by this point, so chances are, I'm thinking none of the above, but something makes me turn to my brother and ask him, 'Are you going to be there when this all disappears? Because it's going to . . .'

I know, I *know* . . . how to stop a party in its tracks, right? And, to this day, more than a decade later, I don't know where those dark thoughts came from. Because that night in February 2002 when we won our first Brit Award and were riding so high, I had no way of knowing what a path of highs and lows we were already on. It didn't occur to me how much money would pass through our hands, how many millions of pounds we'd make for other people, while all four of us would end up scraping around to pay our bills. I couldn't have guessed how much of our personal lives would become tabloid fodder for a press determined to bring us down, or how we would become accidental witnesses to tragedy, and then be engulfed in a media storm that nearly broke us before we'd begun. Nor did I realise how our friendships within the band would be challenged by living together in a bubble, and then having it burst when we least expected it.

All I sensed then, because my dark angel told me, was that we were a group of four young men who would in many ways be tested. And I was right.

CHAPTER 1

'ALL RISE'

Beginnings, Meetings, Becoming Blue

19 May 1999 – Granada Studios, Manchester

ANTONY

Simon Cowell's voice had that special tone to it even then, like he knew something the rest of us didn't. We were nine lads who thought we pretty much knew it all, waiting to go on stage, sing live on air and make a little bit of pop history, being plucked for stardom on . . . *This Morning.* As you do. But, as we stood behind the curtain listening, and he started spelling out his expectations, we all started to go a bit quiet, and even that joker I'd just met, little Lee with his fringe, stopped horsing around for a minute. Suddenly, it had all got a bit serious.

Lovely Caron Keating, a very familiar face who'd been extremely nice to all of us since we'd arrived that morning, had asked Simon Cowell exactly what he was after. Without hesitation, he explained, 'There's got to be a chemistry there, you're trying to find people with star quality. All of these guys, I presume, can sing and dance, but that little extra something . . .'

No pressure then, lads, and if we'd known who he was, or would go on to be, we might have been even more nervous. But Simon

Cowell wasn't Simon Cowell back then; he seemed like just another music industry exec. in a baggy, checked shirt, with a big grin and a pretty special haircut. It was Kate Thornton sitting next to him who was actually more intimidating; after all, *Smash Hits* was our Bible growing up and she'd been its editor. And, never mind all that, we were about to appear on *This Morning*, the show we'd all watched for years, as it set about creating its very own boy band.

We'd all got through previous auditions to get this far, but this was different: we'd be singing live on TV, no backing track, no musicians, just our voices in all their naked glory . . . or instantly apparent lack thereof.

Despite Simon Cowell's certainty that day about exactly what it was he was after, it seems only right to point out that it was actually Kate Thornton who first mentioned the phrase that would go on to launch a billion-dollar franchise on both sides of the Atlantic and would turn Simon into the global TV powerhouse he became. She said: 'It's an indefinable X factor that sorts out the wannabes from the superstars and that's really what we're looking for.'

Bang! See what I mean about falling into history? Little did we know . . . It's really hard with hindsight to say if any of those waiting behind that curtain had that '*je ne sais quoi*' they were going on about, but it was a motley crew indeed. There were some faces I already knew, and others whose paths would later cross ours for years to come. There was Declan Bennett, who used to be in a band called Point Break before he later turned up as Charlie Cotton, Dot's grandson, in *EastEnders*. Another lad was Andy Scott-Lee, who later appeared on *Pop Idol* and made it all the way to the final. His sister Lisa was also in Steps. Those wannabe tiers of the pop industry made for a small world in those days, with everybody knowing everybody else, usually from queuing up for hours together at different auditions. Two people stood out for me. One was a lad from Exeter called Will Young, who seemed pretty confident in two vests and big trainers.

He stood up tall and looked everyone straight in the eye, and he sang an excellent version of 'I'll Be There', getting his voice nearly as high as Michael Jackson's. The other one was that joker I told you about, a bloke called Lee Ryan, who I had a laugh with, talking about our favourite TV programmes. He had blond curtains for a haircut, and was wearing a suit! He looked like a dodgy best man or a car salesman, and that suit was easily two sizes too big for his adolescent frame. He told everyone he was 16, but I wasn't exactly sure about that.

LEE

Okay, so I was actually 14, but I always liked a suit. For this audition, I'd chosen an impressive silver number, only slightly too large, that I'd found in a Greenwich clothes shop. Funnily enough, behind the counter that day had been one Dave Berry, later to follow his own star in the entertainment industry.

I hadn't actually applied for this audition myself, it had been my Aunty Joan who'd sent my demo off on my behalf, and she'd fibbed about my age. But I'd been to stage school so I wasn't nervous about performing at all, so I was getting ready to sing 'Swear It Again' by Westlife. Out of everyone there, I got on best with Antony – we didn't stop talking, and he was making me laugh, which is pretty much all that matters at that age, right? Then he went on before me, and I heard them ask his name, and he said, 'Michael from Edgware' and I thought, 'Hold on a minute, is anyone here actually telling the truth about themselves?'

ANTONY

To this day I can't explain what happened there. The only reason I can think of is that my chosen song was 'Outside' by George Michael, and I got a bit tied up in knots. Anyway, I started singing. No,

YouTube doesn't lie . . . Yes, I was wearing a shirt long enough to be a nightdress, and white baggy chinos. And if that look was a bit too ordinary for the judges, they couldn't fail to be bowled over by my enthusiastic headshakes and some serious thumb action. All those hours in front of the mirror had not been wasted.

Except they had! At the end they called out some names, and you may be amazed to learn that neither the thumbs nor the rest of my performance made the cut. Lee did get through (as did Will Young), so I wished him luck, we swapped numbers and said we'd stay in contact.

LEE

Nothing much happened with the band, although it obviously planted a seed in Simon Cowell's brain. The whole idea of forming a boy band live on TV like that hadn't been done before, but he saw all the potential, took that concept and ran with it. We just happened to be there on day one and become his accidental prototypes.

More significant for me that morning, as it turned out, was making a friend of Mr Antony Costa. We stayed in touch, more than you'd expect teenage blokes to bother, really, keeping tabs on each other's progress, sharing tips for auditions, having a laugh. And then, two years later, I got a phone call, and it seemed our paths were about to cross once more . . .

ANTONY

Have I mentioned George Michael already? He was my hero, the backbone of my musical education growing up – him, and *Cabaret*, naturally. I was pretty ordinary at everything at school – the teachers knew it, *I* knew it – but I didn't mind, because that was the musical they put on one year – a bunch of 14-year-old North Londoners acting out the tale of a 1930s' Berlin nightclub against the background of the Nazis' rise to power. It seemed completely normal at the time. Not sure I got every single subtext in the story, but I certainly caught the singing bug, and that was it, I'd found my thing.

Occasionally, I could be prised out of the house for a football match with my mates, but otherwise, I spent all my downtime hollering into my hairbrush in front of the mirror. Of all the stars of the day, for me it was always George, which, as a fellow Greek lad from North London, seemed only right and proper. Which meant that the locals in pubs around Edgware, Stanmore and Barnet were treated to more than their fair share of 'Faith' and 'Father Figure' when I turned 17 and started my own tribute act. Yes, you read that correctly. And if you should have happened into Edgware's Masons Arms of a Friday night around that time, you would no doubt remember being treated to the sight of a wobbly but keen singer in the corner – double denim and aviator glasses, the works.

By then, I was always reading *The Stage*, and always gigging. I saw it as my apprenticeship. It's all changed now, of course – these days, you can go on *X Factor* and, if you play your cards right, become a star overnight. That's obviously great, a massive shortcut, but if you don't have to put in the hard yards to learn your trade, I'm not sure you appreciate success in the same way when it does come. And you'd definitely miss out on the fun of the early days. Come on, who wouldn't want to wear double denim, singing to seven people, and possibly a dog, in the Masons Arms of a Friday evening?

For me, if the wind was blowing in the right direction and blew some generous types through the doors, I'd make £50 for my pains and I thought I was winning. And then I got blown in a fortunate direction myself. I used to like practising my new songs by doing karaoke, which was how I ended up in a bar called The G-Spot in Golders Green. They had karaoke every Friday, and this bunch of lads I'd never heard of used to turn up for the same reason. I'll be honest, I thought they were all a bunch of berks, ripping their tops off and posing around, but one of them was always polite and much nicer to me than the rest.

DUNCAN

My friends in North London always suggested we went to The G-Spot on Fridays, because that was karaoke night. And we'd be there, hanging out, and there was this lad called Antony doing his thing, and they just weren't sure about him. I really liked him, used to talk to him whenever I saw him, but they thought it was weird, him turning up every week with his dad.

ANTONY

My dad used to come with me because I couldn't drive. I was still only 17. My whole family knew what I wanted to do, and as far as my dad was concerned, if it meant I wasn't hanging round street corners and starting trouble, he'd support me in all of it.

He even bought me a PA system for my birthday – a microphone, amp, sound-desk, the works – and started doing the sound for me whenever I got a gig. Bless him, he was absolutely useless, but we did have a laugh.

DUNCAN

I used to like that about Antony and his dad, the idea of them sticking together. I used to watch them joking, trying to work their equipment, and, in fact, it touched me more than he would have realised, because I'd grown up without a father, and I'd recently lost my grandfather, who'd always played that role for me.

My mother brought me up on her own and she was away a lot,

working shifts as a nurse, so I spent huge amounts of time with my grandparents. Grandpa was the most important man in my life growing up, so I was lucky he was such a special person. He'd been a colonel in the army before he retired and became a music teacher, so as well as everything else he did for me, he introduced me to music. We lived in Blandford Forum, an old army town, and every weekend, Grandpa would play the piano in the church at the garrison, and I got to go with him. For a seven-year-old, it was the highlight of my week, driving up to the gate, where the guards in uniform asked to see Grandpa's pass, which said 'lieutenant colonel'. Then they saluted him, raised the barrier and we were through. It was unbelievably cool, and then I'd sit next to him in the church, while he played.

I'd played the piano myself since I was four, he made sure of that. But despite Grandpa instilling his own love of tunes in me, I wasn't really allowed pop music in the house – Grandma said it used to hurt her ears. We had a really old stereo, and I used to sit tucked away in the corner, hoping she wouldn't notice I was listening to the Top 40 with headphones on. Kylie Minogue was my favourite – I had a poster of her on my wall. No, I'm not expecting this to surprise you. The benefit of hindsight, eh?

Ours was a pretty religious household – my first performances as an altar boy remain among my best work – so I thought I'd pulled a masterstroke with the first ever record I bought. How could Grandma object to Enigma with all that Gregorian chanting at the beginning? I did get to play it a couple of times before it was whisked away.

The only thing more glamorous to me at the time than organ bashing at the garrison was Butlins, where my mum took me on holiday when I was little. *Hi-de-Hi* was my favourite television programme, and I was in love with Su Pollard. I adored the Redcoats and was determined to be one myself. And I managed it, reader, signing on for singing duty with Haven Holidays in Bridport and staying for a year. I loved it, especially dressing up as a cat and singing 'Memory'. Fine times!

As with the others, *The Stage* magazine was my Bible, and I used to audition for anything I spotted. I was pretty lucky, getting into two bands in swift succession, which meant moving to London.

The first was a boy band called Volume 5, which, you're right, sounds like a hairspray. We lived in Oxford Street in bunk beds in our manager's apartment, and were – how to put this nicely? – shit. But we were all together and the most exciting thing we ever did was turn on the Walthamstow Christmas Lights.

My next band was Tantrum, three boys and two girls, built on the whim of a rich man who wanted us to sing songs for his girlfriend. There were some familiar faces in the auditions – Myleene Klass made it to the shortlist – as well as in the final line-up. Among us was Rita Simons, who played Roxy Mitchell in *EastEnders*, Ziggy Lichman, who went on to be in the band Northern Line, before turning up as Zac in *Big Brother*, and a bloke called Jonas. Years later, I turned on Channel 5 one day and there he was, reading the news. It's a comfortingly small world.

I was in Tantrum for a year, and we got paid a weekly wage. But we soon realised it wasn't going anywhere, and both my grandparents died during that time. We all knew it was time to move on.

With the money my grandparents left me, I was able to put a deposit on a house in East Finchley and buy myself a bit of time to come to terms with my grief over losing those people so dear to me in such swift succession. I worked as a barman at the Old White Lion in the evening, while by day I was a perfume salesman, standing in the door of Selfridges and spraying people as they walked in. Those two jobs meant I had time to carry on going to auditions in between, and one of those auditions was for a brand new band being put together by someone who sounded like he knew what he was doing.

LEE

Daniel Glatman was a bit of a geek (sorry, Daniel, but you were), very young, but definitely a man on a mission. As he later told it to us, he walked into the record label's offices, announced, 'I want to put a boy band together,' and the boss at the time, Hugh Goldsmith, replied, 'Okay, go find them, bring them back, and here's £10,000.' Why can't everything in life be that simple? It was only later Daniel revealed to us that what had actually happened was that he'd somehow blagged his way into Hugh's office, talked a good game until he was blue in the face and eventually been given three months to put a band together, or he'd have to pay the money back.

I'd grown up going to performing arts schools, good ones like Sylvia Young's Theatre School and the Italia Conti Academy of Theatre Arts, thanks to my mum. She had spotted my singing potential very early on, and she'd been keen to give me the best possible chance at a creative future. I was pretty fortunate in that way – one day, she even spotted me doing my homework, told me to stop because she said it was more important that I learned the harmonies to 'Endless Love'. It turned out she was right. Years later, I ended up sharing the stage with Lionel Richie, singing another one of his classics, 'Easy', so I guess my mum pushed me in the right direction, encouraging my love for all things Motown.

Something else she passed on to me was being a big softy even as a teenager – I once gave away a pair of new shoes to a bloke at a tube station and my mum didn't even tell me off – but I was also pretty headstrong, certain that I knew it all. I'd walked out of school aged 15, thinking I'd learned everything I was going to need – somehow, I had a good idea that algebra wasn't going to feature largely in my future. I wasn't afraid of work, and used to make my money with all sorts of jobs – on a stall, on a roof, anything to make a pound note. But the musical seed had been sown, and I also used to go every week to the newsagent to pick up my copy of *The Stage*.

It's so strange to talk about, now everything and everybody is available on the internet, but back then, if you didn't have an agent, reading the ads at the back of *The Stage* was the only way to spot what was going on, and for management and record labels to find you. That's how bloody old we are!

DUNCAN

I'd sent in a picture and a demo tape, and was invited in to meet Daniel. He was young but looked older, and seemed intent on doing well in the industry.

People seemed to be trickling in and out all day. I got up on stage and sang 'Can't Help Falling In Love' by Elvis, and then channelled my inner Redcoat with Michael Ball's 'Love Changes Everything'. Not perhaps the most cutting-edge choices, but hey, I got a call back and was invited to a singing lesson, where I spotted my old pal Antony, and met Lee again. We'd crossed paths at a previous audition but hadn't really talked.

My first memory of Lee that day was of his massive, brick-sized phone, and he was arguing with somebody on it. That call obviously ended badly, and he went bonkers, head-butted the phone and then threw it on the floor, where it smashed into a million pieces. He stared at it for a minute, then he looked at me and said, 'Can I borrow your phone?' I guess he started as he meant to go on.

He was very smartly dressed, though – I'll give him that – all nice jeans, smart black shoes, Ben Sherman shirt . . . My influences had been my skateboarding pals back in Devon, so I had a bit of a baggier thing going on.

LEE

Duncan had on some truly dodgy shirts. He was a bit of a hippy back in those days and his dress sense was terrible – who wears tracksuit bottoms an audition? Has it improved now? I'm always optimistic. With Dunc, though, it was all about the hair. There was loads of it, hanging over his face, as this little pretty boy was sitting in the corner. He looked a bit stand-offish, but he was probably just shy. And he wouldn't lend me his phone.

ANTONY

Daniel was happy that Duncan and I already knew each other, so that worked in our favour, and we were the first two to be picked. Then he asked Lee to join, plus two other blokes, Richard and Spencer. Richard was actually one of the lads Lee and I had met during our appearance on *This Morning*. As well as sharing that strange baptism of fire, he was friendly, very funny, and we all got on well with him. Spencer was a bit more competitive, and, being young lads, we butted heads with him occasionally. Don't get me wrong, he was a nice enough lad, but we just never really clicked.

DUNCAN

The three of us became really tight with Richard. One of the best times was when we spent a weekend at his family home in Westbeach, where we went out together on jet skis, sang karaoke in a local bar and his mum cooked us all lovely food. They couldn't have been more welcoming, and Richard was incredibly good fun, really engaging. But I can't say we connected with Spencer in the same way. However, despite most of us getting on so well, it just didn't work. Something about that line-up simply didn't feel right, but none of us said anything, until the day came for us to sign our contract with Virgin Music [10 September 2000].

We were literally in the car on the way there, my phone rang, and it was Daniel. He said, 'We have a problem. You, Lee and Antony need to get out of the car, make an excuse and get here by yourselves without the other two. I don't know how you're going to do this, but you'll find a way . . .'

It was ridiculous. I had to make up some excuse about the lawyer not being happy with the contract, saying it would happen the next day, while I was frantically texting Antony and Lee and telling them to meet me up the road. Somehow, the right people got to the Virgin offices, and our management was waiting. They put us on the spot, saying, 'We love you three, but we weren't happy with the other two. If you're happy to sign, we can make this work, with someone else. Are you happy to sign?', with the pen hovering in the air.

Friendship has always been really important to me. Because I'm an only child, my friends are my extended family. The idea of letting Richard down like that was terrible, and Antony and Lee felt the same. Funnily enough, we weren't so bothered about Spencer – he'd been a cocky time bomb waiting to go off, and we'd already had a word with the manager about him. But Richard's abrupt exit made us feel awkward. However, at that point, you're also feeling so grateful that it's not you they've cast away, that they want you, not somebody else, that you just think about yourself, horrible as it is.

LEE

I know what you're thinking: if somebody being too cocky was the problem here, why was I still in the band? Well, I have to be honest, I think wearing a cap saved me. Bear with me . . .

I used to wear caps all the time I was at school, and one thing I learned pretty fast was, when you're in trouble, put your head down and shut up. I knew those two guys, Spencer particularly, were over-stepping the mark. One day, Hugh Goldsmith walked into a meeting with us, and they started talking over him, and I saw his face change, and I just knew. I thought, 'That's it, it's all over,' and I pulled my cap down, put my hands in my pockets and just shut up. Which proved to be the right decision, because almost the very next day they were out. (Perhaps I should have made sure I was wearing a cap the day we were interviewed by *The Sun* about 9/11, but that's another story . . . And the whole time I was in the *Celebrity Big Brother* house, come to think of it, but that's another story, too.)

DUNCAN

So we signed with our hearts in our mouths, and set about trying to find a fourth member. But it proved to be more difficult than we'd thought; we just couldn't find anyone that fitted. We had auditions at Pineapple Studios in Covent Garden, with loads of people coming in from everywhere. It was like *The X Factor* and we were the judges. We got the giggles frequently, with Lee disappearing beneath the table sometimes, but laughs aside, we started to run out of ideas. And then Lee remembered his housemate. One day, he walked in and told us, 'Simon needs to be in the band, he's great.'

SIMON

I'd first met Lee at an audition for another band, ages before, and Duncan had actually been there, too. The very first time I walked into a room with them in, Lee was playing pool and being loud and boisterous. 'He looks like trouble,' I thought. (Sorry, Lee!) And Duncan was sitting on the floor, legs crossed, with floppy hair covering his face – the whole Brad Pitt-a-like thing going on. And then he started singing, and I noticed his husky voice, and then it was Lee's turn and I thought, 'Wow, I want to be in a band with you!' Nothing came out of that day, but Lee and I stayed in touch.

LEE

Simon stood out straight away because he was very good-looking. It was no surprise for us to learn he was also a model. His body was ridiculously toned, and he had this bleached blond hair. You just knew when you met him that he had this star quality about him. He still has it, but we're a bit more used to it now.

SIMON

I was at a bit of a crossroads in my life that day. Back in Manchester, the year before, I'd won a modelling competition for *Pride* magazine, which meant I had a contract, but I had to move to London to be able to start work. I had a girlfriend back home at the time, so I was torn between the two. I've always been independent, and one day a friend said to me, 'Sometimes you have to be selfish to be kind to yourself. You have to be prepared to move on.' And that was exactly what I ended up doing. But it was hard.

However, I didn't join the music industry on that particular day, but I made friends with Lee – who, as I discovered, wears his heart on his sleeve, is very generous and impulsive, but sometimes doesn't have a very good memory. I'd just lost my grandfather and was back in Manchester licking my wounds when he called to see how I was doing. I told him I needed to get to London, but I couldn't work out how I was going to pay for it. Next thing I heard was, 'Just move in with me. My sister's moved out, you can have her room.' 'What will your mum say?' I asked. He said she'd be fine, and I remember saying, 'Oh, *will* she? We'll see.'

LEE

Yes, I forgot to mention it to my mum until I got a call from Simon a couple of days later to say he'd got to Charing Cross and would be catching the next bus to Kidbrooke. So, at that point, I thought I'd better say something.

SIMON

Much later, over a cup of tea, Lee's mum told me her version of events, which was that he'd said to her, 'Remember that guy from Manchester you used to speak to on the phone? Well, I've told him he can move in.' She said, 'What do you mean, for how long?' And Lee said, 'He said, he'll see.' She must have thought she had a right cheeky one on her hands. But we got on very well – I kept my room nice, and Lee's mum is one of those special people who puts into action her belief that when you're in a position to help people, you should. We became a cosy little unit, and I ended up staying for six months before I'd saved up enough to move into my own place. I got a job on Scrubs Lane, right across on the other side of London, so my travelling started at six in the morning. I like my sleep, and I was 10 minutes late every single day. But I was also writing songs in my head – during that time I wrote 'Bounce', which ended up on the first album [*All Rise*], and 'Flexin' which appeared on the second [*One Love*]. I had a job, I was living in London, I'd started my new adventure, and so I was pretty happy.

Then Lee got a call from his mate Duncan about auditions for a brand new band, and he asked me if I wanted to come along too. I was worried, and asked him, 'What if I get in and you don't? I'll feel really bad because you've helped me out so much already.'

His mum was listening to our conversation, and later she said to me, 'Thank you for not jumping on that, like so many people would, you're a true friend to my son.' And I was, as he was to me.

It turned out no one needed to worry about split loyalties. Lee was straight in as soon as he started singing, but I didn't get along with Daniel Glatman the way the others did. He was a great bloke, but we just didn't gel. He was only a couple of years older than me, and I still had a lot of Moss Side attitude. I found it really difficult to even listen to what he was saying, let alone follow his instructions.

So that was that, Lee was off with the rest of them, and I sat back to lick my wounds until a few weeks later, he came home to say the line-up had changed and now it was just him, Antony and Duncan, while they looked for a fourth. He tried to persude me to go again, but I told him, 'I don't think so, man, that's not going to work. I've already burned that bridge, sorry.'

LEE

They tried out all sorts of different people, including one bloke who was perfectly nice, but he was even younger than me, and I just kept thinking Simon would be better. I admit a part of me was thinking, 'Hang on, I want to be the baby.' But I knew Simon would be great – he wanted to be in a band, he was always writing songs and asking me for techniques on how to improve. Whenever we practised together, I could hear he had this amazing tone; there was real natural talent there, he just sounded unique. I heard it and, young as I was myself, I could tell there was something special there that could be developed if he had the right people around him. So I was crossing my fingers.

SIMON

I'd made some other friends in London by then, and I was hanging out with a girl called Ruth – just friends, but very close. And a couple of days after my chat with Lee, she called me. She said, 'A friend of mine is a producer, and he's working for this new band at Virgin. They've already got three guys, and they're looking for a fourth. I've suggested you – would you be interested?'

She had no idea I was living with Lee. These were two completely different pathways that led to the same place. Of course, when Lee heard that, he thought the stars had aligned and it was all meant to be and I must admit, I was pretty persuaded by it myself. So, I headed off for another meeting with their manager, Daniel, and the first thing I did when I arrived was to apologise to him for getting off on the wrong foot.

He looked at me for a while, and then he said, 'You're being a man for saying you were wrong, so why don't you sing something for us?'

'Sure,' I said. 'Anything you like.'

And he gave me 'Flying Without Wings'.

'You have to be joking,' I said. 'This is Westlife.' And off I went again. 'I don't like Westlife, blah blah . . .' Sometimes I just can't help myself. But this time he decided to overlook it.

Antony was the last person I had to meet and he had the final say. Of course, Duncan and Lee had been building me up and Antony, being typical of the man I now know, was resisting it purely for that reason. 'Well, I'll see when I meet him. I'll decide for myself, won't I?'

Lee had given me the heads-up that Antony doesn't like people who look away and have a lettuce handshake, so the first thing I did was eyeball him and pump his hand like a salesman. He must have thought I was a bit strange. We were still young men, finding out things about ourselves. Meanwhile, the lady in the Virgin offices was giving me fresh problems – she'd decided my long hair made me too pretty; she wanted it cut.

DUNCAN

Justine, Hugh's right-hand woman, actually took me to one side and said, 'Get him to shave all that hair off, it looks terrible.'

SIMON

I'd just paid £700 for a portfolio of model shots, and they all had hair! I was thinking, 'They want me to cut my hair off for the band, and then if I don't get in, that's my modelling gone as well.' Now you may say hair grows, but . . . Most black guys have shaven hair, I was getting work because of my hair, it was my unique selling point. So what should I do?

I took a risk, the hair went, and I went back to the record label's office. The same lady was there, and she did a double take, and said, 'Yes, that'll do.'

DUNCAN

He's being modest. She couldn't take her eyes off him: he had it all going on, the shades, the hair. He looked like a superstar.

SIMON

A week later, I was signed. Three had become four.

LEE

I'm taking all the credit for this, but nobody ever listens to me.

DUNCAN

We didn't have a name for ages. Lee wanted to call us Chenise, but fortunately nobody ever listens to him. Turned out it was the same name as his mum's hairdressing salon. For God's sake . . . I liked the name Four Souls because it had depth, but Antony made the valid point that we were clearly asking to be called Four Arse Holes, or Fore Skins. Either way, it could be problematic.

ANTONY

Then, one day, we were on the Underground, on the way to record our very first song. The record company had told us, 'We need a name, you need to come up with something.' No pressure, people . . . We were struggling, and it was turning into a bit of a boring old process.

SIMON

They wanted a name that didn't scream 'boy band', and I was thinking about all these top artists like Red Hot Chili Peppers, Pink, Black Sabbath, and realising they all had colours attached to them.

ANTONY

So we were on the Tube, chewing on it, and Simon suddenly said, 'What do you think of the name Blue?' Why? 'Because we've got to get on that blue line next,' he said. We were all a bit stumped, turning it over in our minds. 'Blue . . . okay.' Lee threw in a 'What about Yellow?' but we pretended we hadn't heard.

As soon as we got off the Tube, we phoned up the record company to tell them, but they interrupted us. They said, 'We think we've found the name for you, boys.' Our hearts sank. What was it?

'It's Blue.'

'But that's our name, we've just thought of it, that's why we phoned . . .'

But they had thought of it as well. Very bizarre . . .

SIMON

We all just looked at each other. Lee started shouting, 'It's a sign, it's our destiny.' Usually, we don't pay him any attention when he starts going all Mystic Meg on us, but even I have to admit, something strange was going on that day. So from then on, we were Blue.

CHAPTER 2

'BUBBLIN'

The Arrival of Huge and Sudden Success

2000

DUNCAN

I was incredibly excited. For years I'd been trying to crack this nut. I'd thought it was completely all over for me at 21, when I was spraying perfume over those lucky ladies in a department store, and instead here I was with a recording contract in my hands.

I was swiftly brought down to earth with a bump when I came home with it, to my house in East Finchley. I was sharing with six other blokes, in a big three-storey house. I ran in to share the news, but at first I thought the house was empty. Then I heard a noise from the top floor, so headed up there. The door was locked, but one of my mates let me in. They were all sitting in a circle, smoking weed, pretty uninterested in my arrival. 'I've just signed my record deal,' I announced to the room at large, hoping someone would twig the enormity of the occasion. My friend Ming eventually did the honours. Popped a champagne cork? Danced around a maypole in the garden? Not quite. 'Cool, man,' he offered before lighting up again. I decided to settle for that.

It seemed they were equally unperturbed by my new daily routine. While they all headed off in the morning to their respective work-places, I jumped into the ridiculous Mercedes that drew up at the door to carry me off in splendour to the studio. I sat in the back, grinning, hoping the neighbours would be twitching their curtains. Of course, I could have gone on the Tube – it would have probably been quicker in the rush hour. And, of course, I only realised much later that it was actually just the bosses' way of making sure I turned up on time, rather than a sign of their appreciation for me.

Despite getting used to such luxury very quickly, I must admit I remained in a state of heightened paranoia for the entire first year of Blue. After witnessing the brisk disposal of two of our founding members, I realised any one of us could just as easily get the chop. I used to phone our manager, Daniel, at least once a week, asking, 'Are they happy with us? Have they said anything?' I'd seen how quickly five had become three, it could easily happen again.

SIMON

Daniel managed us really well from that perspective. We were his very first group, so we were all riding this wave together, but he managed to hide his own enthusiasm and anxiety behind a very unflappable exterior. I'm sure he was getting all sorts of beef from the record company – they'd invested a lot of money in us, and their demands in return landed on his shoulders. But he only told us what we needed to know, and didn't hang either carrots or sticks in front of us, until he'd dealt with it. He left us to get on with the job, if that's what you can call it.

ANTONY

It's an unusual job, but it is work. And we worked. Every day passed like a whirlwind – we weren't thrown in the deep end like today's talent-show winners, we had to graft. At night, we had to get in the van and turn up to pubs and clubs, where you were lucky if there were more people in the crowd than behind the bar. By day, it was off to secondary schools, where we had to act like superstars in front of a bunch of unimpressed kids that had never heard of us. Throw in gym time and photo shoots in between times . . . and somehow slotted into all of that, we had to sit down in the studio to work out exactly what this great new sound was going to be that we were going to offer these unsuspecting young minds.

LEE

If there's one person to credit for finding that sound, it's the producer Ray Ruffin, who sorted us out on our very first day in a music studio. Hit-makers Stargate later arranged our first single and created Blue's chorus-y sound, that anthem-y thing, but it was Ray who did the groundwork. Unlike us complete newbies, he brought with him a huge Motown legacy that had run through his family. His father, Jimmy, had sung the timeless hit 'What Becomes Of The Broken-hearted' while his Uncle David had been lead vocalist for The Temptations during the magical era of 'My Guy'. Ray found his own talent lay in producing, where he achieved huge success. Sadly, like his famous uncle, Ray was to die too young, passing away in his forties in 2013. To this day, when I sing 'If You Come Back' and 'Too Close' I feel his presence next to me, shouting 'Platinum, baby.' I owe him a huge musical debt. He taught me how to record in the studio and take my voice to places I wouldn't have dared before. Soul was in his family's bones, and he brought it out of ours.

As well as all the pop music around me growing up, I was always singing along to Motown songs, the masters like Marvin Gaye, as well as The Eagles and Elton John. Later, I admired groups like Backstreet Boys and Boyz II Men. They're completely different from

31

each other, but what these two bands shared was harmony. For that to work, you can't have four voices all doing the same thing, you have to find your own spot, and that's what we did: Duncan was low, Antony was husky, I was up high and Simon just sounded rich.

SIMON

Err . . . Duncan was actually breathy and husky, kind of rocky but with a soulful twist to it. Antony had been impersonating George Michael for so long, he had a soft, silky thing going on – back then, anyway. And I still remember the first time I heard Lee sing; I thought, 'I'm going to make a lot of money with that boy.'

DUNCAN

I was stunned. My first thought when I heard Lee sing was, 'How can a voice like that come out of a person like this?' (Sorry, Lee, but I do mean that as a compliment.) He had this most incredible, rich sound that was really high, but also strong and powerful. At the time he was 16 and spoke like someone from the market, and it didn't add up for me.

My second thought was, 'How can I possibly compete with it?' I was confident in what I had, and I'd been in a boy band before where I was the lead vocalist and basically sang everything, but now I realised it was game on.

LEE

Nobody has ever pushed me the way Ray pushed me. When we recorded 'If You Come Back', it felt like 1,000 takes. I was there for days, and I hurt. But, through Ray, I felt connected to Motown, and that was all I'd ever wanted. So I kept going.

SIMON

I was the weak link vocally, but I brought the writing, and the benefit of knowing your place in the industry. I'd been a tea boy in my cousin's band once upon a time. I'd seen conflicts, arguing over songwriting, and I knew what harm it had caused, so I came into the band with that knowledge.

DUNCAN

Simon was just cool. He brought an urban element to the group. He gave us an R&B feel, that edge we needed, otherwise we'd have just been three white boys trying to sing soul. Instead, we ended up with this blend where we all got opportunities to shine. The format became me singing the first verse, Antony singing the second verse, Lee doing the choruses, and Simon providing the bridge, with a rap or whatever he had up his sleeve.

SIMON

I felt fortunate I could bring that to the table. I'd been rapping for years, listening to other musicians, making up stories, finding rhythms. Never expected it to find a home in a boy band.

ANTONY

I was shocked when we started working in the studio. I thought you'd go in, record a song and go home. I had no idea you'd be there for 11 or 12 hours, going over just a tiny part of it, again and again. Often I felt completely out of my depth, and I never felt good enough compared with the other three. It was funny because this was what I'd always wanted to do, but once I got there, I couldn't relax and enjoy it. Instead, I was in a state of continual anxiety all the time, thinking: 'Are they going to throw me out of the band? When are they going to say I'm not good enough?' On the outside, I stayed being the cheekie chappie I've always been, doing silly voices, having a giggle, but deep down I was worried, and that lasted for years. Every time my phone rang and I saw it was someone from the record company calling, I was convinced this was the day they'd decided I was the weakest link, goodbye.

SIMON

Antony was the most confident of us all, easily – always the first one in the club, the first one to get a girlfriend. When he was single, he bossed it like a lads' lad. When he had a romance on the go, he'd behave like the world's first boyfriend. He was very black and white, and he knew himself from a very early age, while the rest of us were still experimenting.

DUNCAN

The record company adored Ant. Our manager, Daniel, told me early on that they loved his face, the fact that he looked like a bit of a boxer, somewhere between Al Pacino and Robert De Niro. He's Greek but he brought an Italian vibe, the tougher look the group needed.

ANTONY

I definitely wasn't your typical pop star. Duncan was a mini-Brad Pitt, Lee was cheeky but sweet, Simon was so cool . . . I was . . . evolving. Marmite!

DUNCAN

'You do the talking,' were my instructions from the record company, and so I did. Growing up, my conversations at the dinner table hadn't been your typical arguments with your brothers and sisters as I'd spent all that time instead with my grandparents. They'd been through two World Wars, and were proper old school. My upbringing with them had made me old beyond my years, and aware of what I could and couldn't say. It was like I'd been media-trained in my childhood.

And don't forget I'd been a holiday-resort entertainer in a previous life, which was all about keeping people happy. My night-time duties then had been talking to people at tables, never leaving anyone out, keeping everyone happy. So, now I was in a band, I just carried on doing that. The label was blatant in bending us to their different ideas for each of us – Lee, the cheeky boy with the voice of an angel, Simon, a very pretty black man, street boy Antony, and me, all floppy and friendly, with my long hair, talking to everybody all the time, channelling my inner Redcoat.

SIMON

We were all tokens, there to fit an image. Remember how nobody looked at Justin Timberlake properly until he began singing and moving? Well, the same thing happened to Lee, and it made me laugh. He wasn't considered a pretty boy until people heard his voice, and then they started looking at him differently because of how he sounded. And pretty soon, they started looking at him differently because of the stuff he was coming out with in interviews. Whether singing, speaking or sharing his ideas about life, love and the universe, he was always pretty unusual.

LEE

I'm dyslexic and I have ADHD . . . oh, and I'm left-handed. So there's a lot of unusual stuff going on inside my head, which sometimes pops out. I've always had a lot of nervous energy – I have to be doing stuff, I can't sit still for very long, and my attention span is shorter than a gnat's. And I'm just not conventional. But who's to say what's normal – shall we go with eccentric? I'm happy with eccentric.

A couple of years ago we were all travelling together in a minibus in Berlin, and everyone started discussing whether I was medically diagnosable or just everyday bonkers. It seemed everybody had a different opinion, until I ended up having to chip in, 'I am actually here.'

SIMON

There's no doubt we were objectified by our bosses, and later by fans. But that's what you sign up for. 'Once you sign this piece of paper, your lives are not your own,' I was told. I was prepared for it, and I knew how lucky I was. We all did. And we thought, 'If we really want this to be our dream, we need to stick at it, and we need to stick together.'

It may have looked manufactured because of our different looks, but we had a rare understanding between each other. None of it was fake and I think it was that genuine kinship that people responded to.

Duncan was always the clip-board man, our self-designated liaison officer with the management – like a holiday rep, almost. He did enough worrying for all of us. Lee was away in his own little world, but was also inspiring us with his ideas, as well as his talent. Antony was the joker. If anything ever got too tense, he knew how to time a line so that we all cracked up. Me? I was just happy to be there.

ANTONY

Si was incredibly chilled about the whole thing, which was exactly what we needed to calm the rest of us down. We gave out an unusual energy as a group of four people, which was sometimes brilliant, and sometimes caused us no end of aggro. After we were signed in September 2000, we booked our first lads' holiday for the following January. We picked up our first pay packet and headed for the Mediterranean. When we got there, the lads wanted to rehearse but I thought that was a bit precious, singing into hairbrushes in a holiday apartment in Tenerife. So instead we headed down the road. No one knew us, but people started staring at us walking down the street. All of a sudden, we had random blokes wanting to fight us, I kid you not, because apparently we looked like a boy band.

SIMON

I was more streetwise than the other three, so I told them to keep their heads down. That didn't last long. Soon, we were surrounded by 14 blokes, compared to our meagre four (and one of them was Duncan). I should explain. We'd all grown up as fans of the TV series *The A-Team* and, since our earliest days together, had given each other different characters from the show. Lee was clearly 'Mad Dog Murdock' while I became, inevitably, 'B. A. Baracus'. Antony, always organised, was happy being dubbed 'Hannibal Smith', which left . . .'The Face', a character famous for using his charm, but never his fists, to get out of a bind. So that was Duncan – who else?

Fortunately, this bunch of upstarts had no weapons on them, but they were mouthy, and it soon turned to physical violence. They tried to separate us, but somehow we kept together, and it turned out to be a defining moment for us as a group.

ANTONY

Some geezer started chasing me with a belt . . . fun times.

SIMON

I remember Antony laughing while he was running, and Duncan getting hit, saying, 'Hey, man, there's no need for this.' You could see him thinking, 'Not the face, man.' In these situations, some people freeze and they're only out for themselves, but none of us did that, and by the time we went home that night, there was a bond.

DUNCAN

When it was time to create that harmonious pop sound that would become our trademark, we ended up flying off to meet some obscure but well-respected producers in Norway. It was bitterly cold, and we had to trudge through the snow to get to the studio. When we got inside, the producers were waiting for us – Tor Erik Hermansen, Mikkel Storleer Eriksen, Hallgeir Rustan, or, to give them their professional name, Stargate.

LEE

They were by no means massive back then, they were mainly known as re-mixers, but they'd worked with a few bands and were fast gaining a reputation for creating sounds. Their biggest hit in the UK up to that point had been S Club 7's 'S Club Party' a couple of years before. Later, Hallgeir stayed put in Norway with his family when Tor and Mikkel went off to make their fortunes in America. In their studio in Trondheim, though, in those days, it was still three of them working together – that's how old we are. Their incredible era of hit-making with the likes of Rihanna, Beyoncé, Coldplay and everyone else was still years ahead of them, but even during that freezing-cold week in Norway, their skill for putting together sounds in new and exciting ways became really obvious.

They were great at producing our vocals; making us do lots of different things to get hold of our sound. I know lots of tonal tricks now, and that's because of those early lessons with Stargate. I was nervous, but I was really into their magic making – I wouldn't come out of the booth until it was perfect.

DUNCAN

Once, while Lee was in the booth, I noticed some lyrics written out for Hear'Say's single ['Pure and Simple'], which had been recorded for *Pop Idol* back in the UK. It hadn't been publicly announced yet who'd got through to the final group, and the press had really hyped up the mystery, but when I was reading the lyrics in Stargate's studio, I suddenly noticed the names were written down by each part. We were instantly told, 'You can't repeat it, or let anybody know you've seen it,' so I had to keep quiet. But I remember thinking, 'Oh my God, it's Suzanne,' and being really chuffed for her.

SIMON

They were long days in the studio in Norway, and people invariably started messing about, heading off to find coffee, but I was really interested in how they made their sounds, so I kept walking back into the studio.

The Stargate guys were listening to Pink's debut album [*Can't Take Me Home*], with big tones on it, and they were making similar drum sounds, when I walked in and started singing, 'One for the money and the free rides . . .'I carried on, 'It's two for the lies that you denied.' Out of nowhere, I piped up, 'All Rise. All Rise.' They turned round. 'What did you say?' Tor suddenly shouted, 'Slamming, man.' Next minute I was being eased out of the room, my work apparently done. Later, they called me back for a rap for it, and that was it, the birth of my strange song about a romance gone wrong built around the framework of a courtroom trial.

DUNCAN

We recorded lots of songs with them and 'All Rise' was my least favourite. They made us do some very bizarre things to create that song. They had us marching while we were recording our parts, like we were troops in some totalitarian regime. They kept shouting, 'Sharper, crisper!' So of course, being us, we started taking the mickey. We were cracking up, but we went with it, even though I hated the beat they added.

LEE

They made us all sound punchy and staccato, which wasn't what we thought we wanted. But they were the organ grinders, we were merely the monkeys, and their trained ears could hear it. It's like cooking: we were watching all the individual spices going in, but we had no idea what was going to come out of the oven.

DUNCAN

A couple of weeks later, we were back in England and our record label bosses phoned us up, saying, 'We've got your first single.' We thought it would be just about any of the others, until they announced, 'It's "All Rise".' I said to the others, 'This is a disaster.'

I like to think I have a good ear for music, and I couldn't understand how they could like it. But we went into the office to listen and sat down. A completely unrecognisable tune started playing, and it sounded amazing. Where had that accordion on the intro come from? Where were all the thuds I'd hated? It turned out they'd only put the beat on the track to regulate our vocals then they'd removed it later to make it sound all soft again. HOW had they worked all that out in the studio with us messing about, pretending to be soldiers? It turned out Stargate knew what they were doing after all – who knew?

DUNCAN

My first glimmer of what life was going to be like came in the middle of 2001, several months after we'd signed. 'All Rise' had just come out, and the record company asked us to attend the Smash Hits Tour Show at the Hammersmith Apollo. We hadn't promoted anything at that point, so we were pretty much the only ones who knew we were in a band. Atomic Kitten, Westlife and Co were all performing, we were just wandering around. Well, we turned up, went in, got mobbed. Yes, that really happened. It was a very weird feeling, with girls running up to us, asking for autographs, even though they didn't know our names! We managed to splutter, 'We're Blue, we're releasing something soon, keep listening.' While we were speechless, our bosses just looked chuffed, like they'd known all along.

ANTONY

There was definitely chemistry between the four of us, the sum being much bigger than the parts, and it translated into the music. 'All Rise' ended up selling 200,000 copies, not bad at all for a first single, and even the critics, usually snobby about pop music, had plenty of good things to say about the way our different voices worked together, our so-called 'silky harmonies', and, of course, that surprise accordion on the intro – all our own idea by now, obviously.

DUNCAN

We didn't coast, though, we weren't allowed to. We went on a charm campaign, meeting music journalists and tabloid press, performing at these so-called intimate showcases, where reporters can be persuaded to come for a free glass of bubbly if they'll lend one ear to the new hopefuls crooning at the other end of the room.

ANTONY

The record company had taken a chance and released a CD with only the song's title on the cover, no pictures. So no one knew who we were. In the car one day with my mum, I heard the DJ asking, 'Who are Blue? Are they Swedish? Are they American? Are they German? If you know these guys, we need to hear from you.' Once they realised we were from just down the road and they could just phone us up, it was chaos.

DUNCAN

It was at a Virgin Records showcase party that Nick Lazarus, then running *The Big Breakfast* show on Channel 4, took a massive chance on us. By then, the bed had become an integral part of Big Breakfast, where the presenters of the show would invite their guests to jump on it, or sometimes in it, for a cosy chat. Nick became our champion, saying, 'I love the boys, I love the music, I want to break them. Get them on the bed.' He didn't just book us for a promo slot, he gave us a whole week. And that's what we did. That's when it all changed, when girls came up to us, asking, 'Were you on the telly this morning?'

ANTONY

Two other blokes who gave us a massive leg-up are TV producers Phil Mount and Michael Kelpie. They booked our very first live gig – singing 'All Rise' for *SM:TV Live*. Around that time, I happened to get off the Northern Line near my home in Edgware, just around school finishing time, and somehow I ended up getting chased down the street, on my own, by people I'd never seen in my life.

How do you know you've arrived? For me, it came later, watching telly at home. *Only Fools And Horses* has always been my favourite programme; I've watched it all my life. It was one of the last ever episodes, and Del Boy was reversing into a parking space in the market. As he was driving, Trigger was saying, 'This way, Del' and I could hear a song playing in the market background. And I realised it was us. In *Only Fools And Horses*! That was it.

SIMON

For me, it was appearing on *Top of the Pops* ['All Rise', spring 2001], but I couldn't enjoy it. I could sing all day behind closed doors with the boys, but when it came to performing live, I had no confidence in my voice. My tone would change; I'd sing some words wrong. The boys always said it sounded fine, but I didn't believe them. And *Top of the Pops* was the worst time of all. When I brought myself to watch it back, I realised all the other boys were singing live, but my vocals were from the record. The good news was I was so quiet, the editors had been able to add my voice. The bad news was this was *Top of the Pops*, the show I watched growing up, filmed at Television Centre, which I always passed on my way to football practice. Why did it go wrong? I had too much riding on it – my mum watching, everyone in Moss Side going to see me. I was convinced they were going to start taking the mickey when I next saw them. Perhaps I was over-thinking it, as I am prone to do.

LEE

The first time I heard us on the radio, we were at a festival, and we all started screaming. It was everything I'd imagined as a kid, all those years I'd sung along to Boyz II Men songs. Now here I was, on the same radio, with people singing along to us. My mum had been visiting a medium all my life, and this lady had told her years before that I was going to be a singer and be in a famous boy band. For myself, I'd dreamed about this moment, and I do believe, if you pray for it, and believe in something enough, it will come.

ANTONY

We couldn't be brought down to earth at that point. We were on our way to a festival in Brighton with our tour manager, Johnny B, when all four of us heard 'All Rise' on the radio at the same time. We'd pulled up to the lights and there was a builder's van next to us. We could hear our song on his radio, so we all popped our heads out of the sun roof and said to him, 'Do you like that song?' What a bunch of berks! He answered, like it was a completely normal conversation to have at the traffic lights, 'It's all right.' We shouted in unison, 'It's us!' He said, 'Bollocks,' and drove off. That was when I thought we might have a shot at this.

LEE

A couple of months later, we released 'Too Close'. We were busy in the studio recording the vocals for 'Fly By' when I was invited to go on the radio and talk to the DJ Dr Fox, who was hosting the

Chart Show. He said to me, live on air, 'How do you feel about getting to number one?' Stunned was the answer.

SIMON

From that point on, it really was a case of, 'Right, now we're off to the races.' That was a heady day. That same time, we'd been invited into our management's office and given an ENORMOUS cheque for our next album. We were all flying as we walked back into the studio that afternoon, work still to be done. Lee was flying even higher than the rest of us, following his chat with Dr Fox, and he went straight into the booth to record his vocal for 'Fly By'. That amazing note you can hear at the end of the song was recorded in his first take. It was an outpouring of euphoria that we all share to this day, and it's so good to know it was captured forever on tape. I looked through the glass at this talented young man singing his little heart out and I thought, 'I'm so proud of you.'

CHAPTER 3

'IF YOU COME BACK'

Eyewitnesses to Tragedy

September 2001

ANTONY

Recounting our memories of 9/11 always seems strange, sometimes uncomfortable, even now. So many people suffered on that day that we will never get to hear about, and yet the four of us continue to be asked for our experiences of it. So this chapter in our lives is shared in the full awareness that our fear, pain and trauma are forever dwarfed by those whose stories we've heard, and some whose stories we may never hear. The only comfort in relaying it completely here for the first and only time is hoping it will answer fully all those questions people still naturally want to ask. So, here we go . . .

As soon as 'Too Close' went to number one, we set about preparing to release our third single, 'If You Come Back'. We were pulled into a meeting in our record company office on the Harrow Road to be told, 'For this video, boys, we think you should film it in New York.' As an afterthought, the bosses asked, 'How do you feel about that?'

I was 20 years old and I'd made lots of hops to Europe by then, but I'd never been to America, and neither had the other lads. We were beyond excited.

DUNCAN

I called my mum the day before we were set to leave. We've always spoken pretty much every day, and she always knows what's going on in my world, so she'd got used to hearing about glamorous trips here and there. Nonetheless, at that point she was working as a nurse in a residential care home, and the thought of her son jetting off to film in Manhattan still seemed absurdly exotic, as it did to me. When we spoke that day, she told me a friend of hers had said the best view of the city was from the top of the World Trade Center so I promised to go up there and take a photo for her to show him.

ANTONY

On 10 September, we flew to JFK International Airport from Heathrow, and we were put in business class seats. It was the first time I'd ever watched a film on a plane. Even by the standards we'd got used to over the preceding months, we were being treated like princes, and we spent the journey revelling in our good fortune.

We arrived there in the afternoon and went straight to a chat with the director of the video. Our videos were always about two things – locations and haircuts. This time was to be no different – all the usual stuff, us glowering at the cameras, singing our different bits – but this time with a glamorous Manhattan backdrop. We went off to have some clothes fittings, some food, general chit-chat, all the time pinching ourselves that we were actually in New York.

LEE

I'm a massive film buff, and the city was everything I'd hoped it would be, absolutely beautiful. But my head was in a strange place. I was convinced there was a weird atmosphere in the air, and I kept telling the boys, 'Something's not right.' It sounds ridiculous, but I kept seeing the number 1939 in my mind's eye, which got me thinking about World War II, and I even said out loud that I feared something similar could happen again.

SIMON

I'd love to say he's making this stuff up, so many people talked like this later on, but Lee really was distracted by the number 39 that week and sure enough, we kept seeing it everywhere. It became a running joke after we went to a diner on that first afternoon, Lee picked up a yogurt pot, started eating from it, turned it round, and it had '39 cents' written on it. He gave us all this big look, but we just laughed and told him to shut up.

Two other things of significance happened to me that day. I have a brother called Straon who I wasn't brought up with – separate families – and our paths hadn't crossed our entire lives because he lived in New York. When I'd been told we were headed there for a trip, I'd contacted him and made arrangements to meet up with him in the city. We managed it that afternoon. It wasn't a long encounter, but it was important and it went really well. The other thing I did that day was to get a tattoo. I'd been humming and hawing over whether to have one for ages, waiting for a sign. That afternoon, still buzzing from meeting my brother, I went and had it done.

DUNCAN

We had to go to bed really early because of the following day's schedule, which suited us because of our jet lag. We were up at five the next morning, the 11th, and had to head straight out. We were staying in Soho, downtown Manhattan, and it took us a good hour to get across the bridge to Brooklyn, where the shoot was due to take place. The whole time, we were looking back at the stunning view of New York, marvelling like a million other gaping tourists at those two towers dominating the skyline across the water. It was still quite dusky and grey when we were travelling. That amazing blue sky that everyone remembers came later.

ANTONY

When we got to Brooklyn, we found the set in an industrial car park right next to the river, so that the director could capture that perfect scenery behind our usual bobbing heads. We were called into Make-up, in the trailer nearby. My biggest problem that morning, or so I thought, was having the hairdresser give me the wrong blade for a shave. It sounds properly ridiculous now, of course, but that was the carry-on, all the usual nonsense. So I was struggling with this huge challenge, when our coordinator, Carol, burst in, saying, 'There's been a plane crash at the Twin Towers.'

I could make no sense of that. For some reason, as she spoke, I visualised something small, a glider or something, low down near the street, so my instant reaction was to say, 'Oh no, that's sad. Is everyone all right?' And just then we heard a massive shout from outside. We ran out, and everyone in our crew was gazing across the river at the stunning view of downtown Manhattan and the World Trade Center. We could see smoke billowing out into the sky from what we learned was the North Tower, where the first plane had already gone in. Then someone shouted, 'It's a plane,' and pointed to the second tower. Our video team, by pure instinct, trained their cameras on the scene as we all watched the second aircraft crash into the side of the South Tower.

SIMON

These were our riggers, our lighting crew, our gaffers . . . All professional men and women, all booked to do a hard but straightforward day's work. And they ended up playing witness to one of the most defining events in their country's history, purely because they'd agreed to film a pop video for a boy band from the UK, one they'd never even heard of. Our view of the Towers, and the tragedy that befell them, was stark − all too perfect. The footage that our team shot that morning ended up going around the world, and bringing audiences glimpses of what we'd seen for ourselves. The random nature of this universe is something I still struggle to get my head around.

ANTONY

At this point, somebody suggested saying a prayer, so we stood in a circle holding hands. We didn't know any of these people, or the words to say, but we wanted to respect everyone's needs. It was peaceful, but there was a bubbling sentiment of rage too. One man started swearing, 'You're not going to fucking defeat, us, man, we're America.' Another bloke yelled, 'That's it, we're going to war.' It was like they all knew something, and we didn't.

We've never been the most clued-up group of people when it comes to world events, and we were singularly ill-equipped to put into context what we'd seen, what we heard. Add to this the fact that none of us had ever visited New York before, and the day before we'd been walking around thinking we were on some glamorous film set. Now, with dust, smoke, screaming, sirens, planes crashing, it seemed as though we'd entered our own, all-too-real disaster movie. It made no sense on any level. It didn't feel real, or rational. It wasn't something we could process or explain to each other. All we could do was feel the shock, anger and fear around us, and it seemed to be escalating.

LEE

People around us continued to yell, until one voice rose above the rest. A man pointed at the Towers, and shouted, 'My wife's in there,' and everyone suddenly went silent. Just terrible . . .

DUNCAN

Looking back now, I think we were all absolutely traumatised by what we saw. At the time, we were just standing still and watching. Nobody spoke.

ANTONY

I had to turn away. At that moment, one of the American guys offered me a cigarette, but I told him I didn't smoke. He said, 'Take it, it will calm you down.' It was the first time I'd ever smoked, but it worked that day, for the rest of the week, and I got hooked forever.

SIMON

I could see the others looking either numb or becoming emotional, but my reaction was different somehow. If I'm really honest, it made me feel strangely fatalistic. I'd met my brother that day, and I knew that everyone in my life knew how I felt about them. It was as though we'd had a sudden inkling that the world really could end at any moment, and it was a time to ask yourself, is everything in your life facing the right way? And I can truthfully say, on that day in 2001, it was. I was resigned, but I wasn't scared. I felt at peace. Perhaps that was just shock having its effect on me, and it does behave differently in every person, but that day was the awakening of a spirituality in me that has never deserted me since.

ANTONY

Inevitably, after a while it became about practicalities and our production team swung into action. There was no question of going back to our hotel, instead a plan was devised to send us to a hotel further along the Hudson River, in upstate New York. The only vehicle we could get hold of was an old mobile caravan, but it didn't matter, we were just happy to be on the move, and we all clambered in. As we got further away from the city, we began to feel safer – until a tyre blew out as we were racing along the freeway, which meant we skidded across the tarmac and nearly crashed off the side of the road. If our driver hadn't been some kind of military driving expert, an ex-marine or something we'd heard, that could easily have been the end of us. The Winnebago had two wheels in the air. Everyone was screaming.

DUNCAN

That was when we got properly scared, as it seemed the fates were stacking up against us, and our chances of getting home quickly were getting slimmer and slimmer. I felt so sad, then, remembering that my mum had told me to visit the Towers, that the news would have got to the UK, and there was no way of letting her know I was okay because all the phone networks were down. I couldn't even get a one-word text to her.

ANTONY

We got to the hotel in a sweet place called Tarrytown, which looked like something out of an old-school American film, all green and clean, and a million miles from what we'd just experienced. We booked into a lovely hotel, for what was meant to be two days, and everyone started to feel better. Unfortunately, we soon learned that nobody was going anywhere, so this turned into a week, and our nerves started to fray once again. Fortunately for me, I had my new 20-a-day habit to keep me busy.

DUNCAN

During that time in the hotel, we drank an awful lot of alcohol to dampen the shock and numb our emotions. There was just nothing else to do, nowhere to go, everyone having the same conversations over and over again about what it all meant, and so much stress. Everyone was on red alert. Everywhere we looked, TV sets were on, either the ABC or CNN, with breaking news, more breaking news, and we couldn't even phone anyone.

It took me three or four days to get a call through to my mum. When I finally managed it, I said, 'Hi Mum, it's me' and there was just silence at the other end. It turned out she was so overcome with relief she couldn't actually speak. She'd been at work in the nursing home when the news had come on the TV. Everyone there knew I was in New York, so they all just stopped and looked at her, and she'd had three days of fearing the worst. So when I got through, she couldn't speak, and neither could I; we both sat, holding our phones in silence.

'IF YOU COME BACK'

LEE

The girls from Atomic Kitten – Natasha Hamilton, Liz McClarnon and Jenny Frost, who had only a few weeks before replaced Kerry Katona – were in the same hotel. They were signed to our label and had also been evacuated from New York. We inevitably spent a lot of time with them; they were all lovely and it was a comfort having them there. That was when Liz and I first got to know each other, and we ended up getting together later. But I had times during that week when I was so scared I would physically crouch down under a table. All four lads slept in the same room the whole time we were there. It felt as though the world had suddenly become completely unpredictable and, by extreme bad luck, we'd chanced upon the wrong place at the wrong time, when anything might still happen.

ANTONY

Finally, a week later, we were able to fly home and, because of our schedule we had to go straight from the airport to a gig in Southampton, an open-air event. The crowd knew we'd be there because we'd announced it on our website, and our families were all travelling down to the coast as well. I'm not by nature a crier, but it was pretty emotional seeing my parents' faces. And being back on stage. Just going through our normal routines felt freshly amazing. I think we all felt very fortunate.

LEE

When we all settled down again in the UK, Liz and I went out for a while after that, and even got engaged. But looking back now, there was no real prospect of us ever getting married, or that relationship working out, nor should it have. It was a strong connection, and we're friends to this day, but it wasn't built on anything like normal circumstances. Instead it was a bond founded on shared fear at an extraordinary time.

SIMON

It's a strange chapter in all our lives, such a massive thing to be part of, when all we wanted to do was sing and dance, and I'm not sure we're any more equipped now to analyse it or put it in any kind of context. But the anniversary of those terrible events will always be important around the world, and we're part of a small group who witnessed them with our own eyes. It will always be a memory of fear, enormous sadness and heaviness. There's no getting away from it. We just carry it with us and, compared with so many others on that day, always feel very fortunate.

CHAPTER 4

'GUILTY'

Made to Feel Very, Very Bad

October 2001

ANTONY

Looking back now, it was clear we'd all been through something significant in our young lives, and no doubt should have taken a bit of time away to take stock, just hang out with our families and friends, and get some perspective. Instead, we plunged straight into fresh rounds of interviews, photo shoots and promo duties for the single 'If You Come Back' – remember that? – which was due out on 12 November, with our first album to follow a fortnight later. We were at a crucial moment in our career, this was the tipping point as to whether we'd make good on all of our management and record company's investment in us, and there was no question of taking our foot off the pedal and giving it less than our all. But we were all extremely tired, even before New York, and absolutely strung out afterwards. We should have known something was going to give.

On 25 October, we made our last trip of the day to the offices of *The Sun* newspaper, to participate in a billed Q&A web chat with fans. Already that week we'd spoken to one magazine after another. Back in the pre-Twitter days, there was no social media to bounce interviews around or keep in touch with the fans directly. We had to sit down with *Top of the Pops* magazine, *Smash Hits*, *TV Hits* and a hundred others, give each of them our all, and hope the reporters liked us enough to give us a fair go when it came to putting our stuff on the page.

It was usually a lot of fun, even if it was the same questions being thrown at us over and over again. Have you got a girlfriend? When's the album out? When are you going to split up? When are you going to get back together? What's the silliest thing Lee's ever done?

DUNCAN

But now they had something else to ask us about . . .

SIMON

How was 9/11?

ANTONY

What was it like being in New York on 9/11?

DUNCAN

How did you feel watching the Twin Towers fall on 9/11?

ANTONY

How do you feel about what happened on 9/11?

THE EARLY YEARS

'I was pretty ordinary at everything at school, but I caught the singing bug, and that was it, I'd found my thing.' (Antony)

'You just knew when you met Simon that he had this star quality about him.'

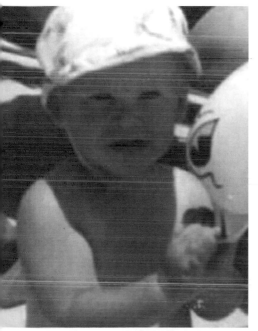

'I think wearing a cap saved me. I used to wear them all the time, and one thing I learned was, when you're in trouble, put your head down.' (Lee)

'I wasn't really allowed pop music in the house – Grandma said it used to hurt her ears.' (Duncan)

THE EARLY YEARS

'I grew up with just my mum, and she was strict.' (Simon with mum Marlene and relative Janet Dinwiddy)

'I spent all my downtime hollering into m hairbrush in front of the mirror.' (Antony)

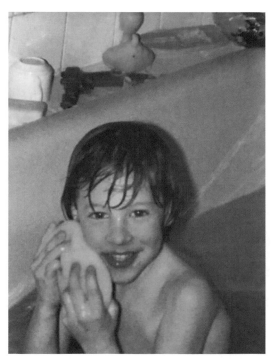

'Friendship has always been really important to me. Because I'm an only child, my friends are my extended family.' (Duncan)

'How do you know you've arrived?'

'Simon suddenly said, "What do you think of the name Blue?"'

ALL RISE 2002–2003

'Is this really happening? We're just four silly lads in borrowed suits.'
(Brit Awards 2002)

'Ever since I was a small child, I'd told my mum how much I wished I could sing with
Elton John. She used to get me to go to bed by saying, "If you pray hard enough…"'
(Germany 2003)

'Simon had it all going on, the shades, the hair. He looked like a superstar.'

'You just felt so liked, loved, appreciated, everyone's mate... It was like living in a warm bubble bath all the time.'

'In early 2003, we got our second Brit Award, this time for Best Pop Act. That sealed it for me.'

THE BEST OF... 2004–2005

'Blue moved as a pack of four wherever we went, so we always had partners in crime for any moments we might suddenly feel shy,'

'We were glued together, but fortunately we never fell ou with each other, we always got on.'
(Capital Radio Party in the Park 2004)

'When we were together, something happened. It was strength in numbers, plus a bit c magic.' (2004)

'Geri was everything I'd hoped she
would be.'

'Friendships in show business are kind of
accelerated...' (Simon partying with Paris
Hilton and Diana Jenkins)

'Stars crossed our paths like glamorous characters in a play. Nobody let us down –
everyone was amazing in their own way.'

'On stage in *Legally Blonde,* with one of my closest friends to this day, the extraordinary Sheridan Smith.'

'Time to show them, Costa. I'd prepared for my role in *Blood Brothers* as all good actors do, watching lots of *Brookside.*'

'Whoopi played games with us all on stage, trying to throw us off our stride.' (Simon appears in the West End production of *Sister Act*)

SIMON

The thing to know is that sometimes Lee just zones out. I've always noticed it – he goes into another world, and it used to happen a lot more than it does now. He tunes in and out, without concentrating. Usually, it doesn't matter because we all chip in with our bits, they kind of make sense, and then he comes in with something funny if he wants to.

DUNCAN

On that day, we walked into *The Sun*'s office in Canary Wharf. We weren't particularly well known, but a couple of people stopped us for autographs on the way in, and everyone was incredibly friendly. We went into a small room, no cameras, just a few people – a young male journalist reading questions from the fans' web chat, and *The Sun*'s showbiz columnist, Dominic Mohan, sitting to one side. And off we went. Nearly home time . . .

After a couple of standard questions, the lad read out one from fans, and it was 'What was 9/11 like?' and I heard Lee sigh. But I thought, 'Here we go, we got asked the question, we know what to say here.'

ANTONY

So I started by saying, 'We saw the second plane crash into the Tower and then the building crumble.' And the lad, bless him, answered, 'You witnessed all that? It must have been scary.'

SIMON

At which point, I said, 'Of course it was scary, it would be. It's the biggest day of terrorism in history.'

ANTONY

And then, from nowhere, our dreamy fourth wheel, Lee Ryan, piped up, 'What about whales?' Everyone, including us, looked at him confused, wondering what was coming next. It was like he was having a completely different conversation from the rest of us. But then he said, 'What about all the wars we don't hear about? The animals that need saving? This New York thing is being blown out of proportion.'

SIMON

I said, 'Shut up, Lee.'

ANTONY

Lee said, 'Who gives a fuck about New York when elephants are being killed?'

DUNCAN

I said, 'Lee, shut up.'

ANTONY

And out of the corner of my eye I saw Dominic Mohan – who'd been sitting to one side, keeping half an eye on his young lad, but basically tapping into his phone – perk up. His journalist's radar had pinged in his ear, and he stopped the Q&A and pulled the young reporter over to him. They had a quick chat then the lad came back, put his recorder on the table and asked, 'Would you mind saying that again?'

LEE

And I just spewed it all out, not just the stuff about whales and elephants, but also about starving children, people dying of AIDS, famines, wars that had been going on for decades around the world, all ignored by the media. Why did I say all of that? Because they asked me. Because I was tired. Because I really did believe in some of that stuff, but it all came out wrong. And because I was 18, and I thought my opinion mattered.

I also added for good measure just in case there was any doubt, 'I'm not afraid to say this, it has to be said and that's why I'm the outspoken one from the band.'

DUNCAN

And that was it. We were a bit surprised, but we weren't too worried. We all just thought, 'Lee's been a berk, but no harm done.' Off home, job done. And then the shit hit the fan.

Our PR got straight on the phone to our manager, Daniel, who hauled us all over to the Virgin offices. Seems it was a bigger deal than we'd realised. The big chiefs were there and Daniel was insisting, 'I don't believe he said that. He's not that stupid.' But the publicist told him, 'Four times. On the record. You're fucked.'

Even the top brass from Virgin were down on their knees, trying to reach out to *The Sun*, but the people at the paper were having none of it. Dominic Mohan had his scoop, he was sharpening his pencil and he was going to run with it. It was too good not to.

ANTONY

The next morning, the paper came out. The good news was Blue had made its first ever front page. The bad news was it looked like it was all over for the band. There it was, up front and centre, a picture of the burning Twin Towers, us, and Lee quoted with the headline, 'F*** New York'.

LEE

I thought, 'I didn't say that.'

DUNCAN

Inside, there was a double-page spread, with Lee quoted, in all his glory: 'What about the whales? They are ignoring animals that are more important. Animals need saving and that's more important. This New York thing is being blown out of proportion. I'm not afraid to say this, it has to be said and that's why I'm the outspoken one from the band.' Ouch!

Normally, the record company would be ecstatic about the prospect of one of their bands landing a double-page spread in *The Sun*, but from how our manager sounded on the phone, it didn't sound like they were celebrating! We were hauled back into the office once more, while our publicists went into damage limitation mode, apologising to all and sundry for what Lee had said, saying he didn't mean it. They issued a statement from him, even pledging to donate all his royalties from our next single to the Two Towers Fund, run by *The Sun* itself.

ANTONY

They decided it would be good for the band to speak out for Lee, saying how upset he was, how his ideas had come out wrong. They wheeled Duncan out to do a lot of the interviews, because he's the most articulate of the four of us, but we all had our bit to do – all except Lee, that is. He'd been banned from speaking ever again, by the looks of things.

SIMON

We'd been booked to appear on the pop show *SM:TV Live* the following morning, but that was immediately cancelled. We thought, 'Bloody hell. In the space of 24 hours, we were up there, and now it's all over.'

ANTONY

It went dark very quickly. My mum ran our fan club, along with Duncan's mum, and we received threats from Americans, saying they would throw anthrax at us. If we set foot in the US, they were going to shoot us dead. It was all pretty scary.

Some Brits were equally hostile. Thank goodness there was no Twitter at the time because the fan mail was bad enough, plus the people stopping us in the street. 'Your bandmate's a cunt, I hope he dies, I hope you all die, you're a bunch of wankers.' The stuff dreams are made of. There was a poll in *The Sun*, asking people to vote on whether Lee should be thrown out of the band. Our manager, Daniel, ended up in hospital for two days with stress-related gastroenteritis.

DUNCAN

When asked about Lee's future with the band, our management released statements saying 'No comment', so they were definitely keeping their options open.

SIMON

It was never an option for us to throw Lee out. We saw exactly how it had happened. That stupid kid should have been sent to his room and told to shut up, not invited to say more stuff by grown adults who knew they were going to stitch him up. Instead, *The Sun* turned Lee into the villain of 9/11. It was a lot to put on the shoulders of an 18-year-old, and I was worried how he would take it. He ended up embracing it in his own way, saying, 'If you think I'm an idiot, I'm going to behave like one.' But we never blamed him for what happened. There was never a cross word about it between the four of us, not one.

DUNCAN

I never blamed him – I saw exactly how it happened and it could have been any one of us. Lee was just the youngest, the most outspoken. But he didn't mean any harm, and we knew that, which was why it was so easy to forgive. If it had been a calculated, premeditated thing, that would have been different, but there was no malice, it was just one in a long line of very innocent fuck-ups, and you end up kind of loving him for it.

He's apologised lots of times, and we know what he's like. We've seen his real heart and it's impossible not to like him. You just have to remind him occasionally to think before he speaks.

ANTONY

'Cross' is the wrong word, and he didn't have anything to apologise for. We were all very, very tired. Throwing him out was never an option. You don't kick a man when he's down – you pick him up and dust him off. It was more a case of it's happened, what shall we do? Split, or carry on? And we carried on.

DUNCAN

We all knew it was much better to stick together and work our way through it. It proved our integrity and tested our loyalty, because there was a massive cry to kick him out, but the three of us were very vocal that it wasn't going to happen. It's one of the many reasons we are so close to this day. Plus, we loved him.

LEE

At the time it was incredibly frustrating because every time I tried to put things right, I got shut up by the record label, which was probably just as well, as I would undoubtedly have dug an even bigger hole for myself. The problem was that although I did have some strong sentiments that what the press were focusing on was misguided, I didn't have the language to express them properly. I couldn't believe I'd become the target of all this hatred. I thought I was just saying what lots of people thought, that politicians were steering us into a war, that the poor victims of the Twin Towers were being exploited, and meanwhile the world was falling apart – but the way *The Sun* pitched it, I was the biggest problem with 9/11. I was just angry about every aspect of it.

I've always realised how terrible it sounds out of context, but now I look back on it, I also find the attention that was paid to me pretty bizarre. I obviously thought my opinion was terribly important, but no one else should have. I was a stupid kid, shooting his mouth off. That platform was far too big for my brain. Why does the country's biggest newspaper think for a minute that's worth putting on the front page, anyway? I guess a mouthy pop star has always made for easy pickings, but still . . .

Of course it affected me, having that level of abuse on two conti- nents coming my way, but probably not as much as it might have done. The truth of the matter was that by the time I joined Blue and went to New York on that fateful day, I'd already seen a lot of horrible things in my life. Apart from the love of my family, my childhood on a rough estate had exposed me to experiences that left me probably damaged, but also battle-hardened. I'd taken lots of drugs at too young an age before I got my head together, I'd threatened people bigger than me, and been threatened by people smaller. As a teenager I'd nearly messed my life up properly and somehow come through in one piece. This latest fiasco wasn't going to kill me.

Months later, we were invited to the Pride of Britain Awards, and as we were walking out across the foyer of Grosvenor House, the PM himself, Tony Blair, turned up and, randomly, asked for a picture with us. I guess he hadn't been reading *The Sun*. I told Daniel, 'I'm not having my photo taken with that man, he's got blood on his hands.' There were loads of press there, the *Mirror*'s 3AM Girls were hovering, but I didn't care. TB had his photo taken with the others, but I just walked off. Naturally, my publicist was having kittens.

I'm not well-educated, I'm often not informed enough to construct a rounded argument, I'm probably not going to be appearing on *The Today Programme* or *Question Time* any time soon, but I have my ideas, and even if a lot of them are half-baked, I will stick up for what I believe in, and I'm not a hypocrite.

ANTONY

So that all happened at the end of October, and all we could do was sit back and wait for the single to come out, see what damage had been done and if anyone was still prepared to buy our music. It was two weeks spent repairing everything – it felt like years.

SIMON

Then the single came out, went to number one, and so did the album a fortnight later.

DUNCAN

Then it felt like we were back on track, but we were all a bit bruised by the experience.

LEE

Everyone had been shouting, 'Wanker, idiot' at me in the street, and then going out and buying our albums. The press could say what they liked, but fans were saying, 'We don't care, we like their music.' On the one hand, this success summed up everything I love about society, that music really does transcend arbitrary boundaries. On the other hand, it made me think there really was no such thing as bad publicity. We were number one, the boys still loved me, and the big bad press couldn't bring me down. So I thought I was infallible, but that came back to bite me.

CHAPTER 5

'THIS TEMPTATION'

Life in the Limelight

2002

ANTONY

'Gentlemen, please stand two metres away from Miss Spears . . .' Those were the clear instructions from the big men in small suits, even while the lady herself was inviting us onto her bed. We weighed up the pros and cons of disobeying the former versus the risk of offending the latter. Guess who we ignored!

It was as surreal as it sounds. Like everyone else, we were big fans of Britney, and so pretty happy when we were invited to attend the premiere of her film, *Crossroads*, in London's Leicester Square. When we got there, we were ushered upstairs into the star's private room, which, naturally, had a bed in it, seeing as it was a cinema and all. Through the throngs of people wandering around looking important, we could see the familiar face of one of the world's biggest stars, and on it, a definite invitation for us all to come a little closer. We didn't need telling twice. What the lady desires, the lady gets . . . and it seemed this particular lady wanted nothing more at that moment, surrounded by 100 people, than to bounce in good company. So that's what we did. She couldn't have asked for more enthusiastic bouncing bedfellows and she was lovely, but her people were clearly keen to see the back of us. So we eventually bounced our way back off the bed, straightened our ties and that was that. Just another day at the office in what had become an increasingly glorious, dreamlike, chaotic chapter in our lives, ever since the success of 'All Rise' had jet-propelled us into that part of the universe where the brightest stars gather.

DUNCAN

The attention on us seemed gentle at first. We were tucked away in a bubble, and although the buzz around us was getting bigger and bigger, we didn't even realise because we were travelling all the time – getting up in the dark, travelling to the airport, flying across Europe, getting in another car, turning up on stage or in a TV studio somewhere, flying back, going to an event, signing stuff, having our hair done for photos, posing, having our hair done again. Our workload had doubled since we'd got to number one with our second single. It was an endless whirl of activity, and lots of attention, but we were kind of quarantined from the bigger din going on outside. Next thing we knew, a tour was announced, and we assumed it would be a theatre tour, but with the album going to number one, that became an arena tour, and then that became a whole week at Wembley, with matinees added due to public demand. At that point, I thought, 'This is crazy.' You pinch yourself.

SIMON

Lee and I had always gone to the same club while we were recording our first album, and it would always be hit or miss as to whether we'd be allowed in or made to stand in the rain, depending on the doorman's mood. Even when we were inside, we could never get a table – neither of us had any money, apart from when Lee's mum kindly treated us

– so we'd lean against the bar staring at everyone, all busy ignoring us. Lee asked me, 'Why doesn't anybody talk to us?' I said, 'Just you wait. They're going to hear your voice, and things are going to change.'

LEE

Next thing we knew, it was straight past the queue, up to the door, table next to the dance floor, free drinks all night, anything and anyone we asked for. It's a ridiculous way to be treated, really. That all changed in a matter of weeks, yet we were exactly the same people.

DUNCAN

Then the din turned into a roar. We couldn't go anywhere without hundreds of people turning up. I remember we once flew to Malaysia, and we learned that our music had got there before we had. Five hundred teenage girls turned up at the airport! We had no idea how big it had all got. It was as though we were wearing blindfolds. I think we all had an element of fear still, but we slowly started realising this record company needed us as much as we needed them. Then, when our second album, *One Love*, went straight in at number one, we started to think, 'Okay, we're safe.' We began to uncoil the spring of anxiety that had been there ever since the day we'd seen our former bandmates, Richard and Spencer, thrown so casually under the bus. Then our third album, *Guilty*, went to number one, and we felt untouchable. I think it's probably fair to say that, by then, we had started to relax a little.

SIMON

We'd never pretended to be innocent as the driven snow. We were four red-blooded young lads who always liked beer and girls, and now we had money in our pockets and invitations beckoning. Some people, as soon as they sign a record deal, become untouchable by the outside world, but we never felt like that. It only takes five seconds to say hello to someone, so we always did, and if there was dancing to be had, hey, let's bring it on! These people who wanted to hang out with us had bought our albums, they'd given us our dream. It was a pleasure to spend time with them. However, because we were always out and about, sometimes it did work against us. Some situations got a bit hairy – after a few pints women wanted to grab us, blokes wanted to fight us. It's not like you're a real person anymore. Lee was the youngest of us, and I'm not sure he always enjoyed the attention.

LEE

Being looked at? I fucking loved it! I thought it was great. It was everyone's dream. I was a megastar in my own lunchbox. I loved everything that came with it – the alcohol, the music, the money, the romantic encounters on offer . . . If anything, I lived it slightly to excess.

SIMON

Perhaps I should say, 'I'm not sure if he "handled" the attention.'

LEE

I drank myself silly. I once picked up a bottle of Jack Daniel's and downed it a single breath, just to show off.

ANTONY

Lee was named 'Shagger of the Year' – two years running, in fact, by *The Sun*'s showbiz column 'Bizarre', 2003 and 2004 – which was a surprise because his patter was appalling. He used to say to girls things like, 'You remind me of my ex-girlfriend' or 'Your eyes are beautiful. Do you mind if I write a song about them?'

LEE

There was a ridiculous number of kiss-and-tells. I can't believe I enjoyed the company of that many more ladies than your average Joe Bloggs, it's just that my little romances always seemed to end up in the papers. My mum took it in her stride. One morning, opening the paper to another intimate revelation about me, she said casually, 'Well, I think we've established you're not gay.'

DUNCAN

Funny you should mention that, because I had more than my share of beautiful women on my arm back in those days and, as we've since learned, it turns out it didn't exactly establish anything resembling the whole truth. It had never occurred to me, growing up, to be anything other than a dedicated lover of the ladies – Kylie on the bedroom wall, remember? – and it was only when I hit my early twenties that alternative ideas presented themselves. Unfortunately, this dawning realisation of my sexuality coincided with Blue's massive success and the ensuing spotlight, which made for a whole load of secrecy and fear along the way . . . But I'll get to that. For now, life was a big honey pot of flattery and attention, and I hopped in along with everyone else.

LEE

I dived in that pot, swam around in it and took a big, happy bite. I knew it wasn't going to last forever, so I thought, 'I'm going to live this up so that even if I die, I've jumped off the highest mountain and laughed all the way down.' And if I'm being honest, at that point in my life the idea of being like James Dean, dying young and becoming a legend, seemed quite appealing.

ANTONY

It was hard to resist for any of us. You just felt so liked, loved, appreciated, everyone's mate . . . It was like living in a warm bubble bath all the time. When I was a kid, I worked at Wembley Market with my uncle, which meant getting there around midnight to set up stall as they were taking down the concert hoardings. One night, Take That had performed and I gazed up at their faces. A decade later, it was our faces on those billboards.

SIMON

For me, on the personal front, something monumental came out of our success, and having our faces everywhere.

Back in the mid-1990s, I'd become a father to a beautiful little girl, but her life was in Birmingham while mine, as you can see, had taken me all over the place, and she didn't know of our connection. As her mother, Nicola, told it, one day in their living room, Blue appeared on the TV, belting out 'All Rise'. And in front of the screen, her little tot, then aged four, was dancing away, following all the moves, in perfect time. It was then Nicola thought, 'It's probably time she got to know her dad.'

And that was how my daughter Alanah properly entered my life. We both love that it came through our dancing, separately but together, to the same tune. And, guess what, she's a choreographer now, so life's gone full circle. But I'm jumping ahead of myself. Back to the billboards . . .

Success, for me, felt far more professional than it did personal. The fame and attention weren't what I lived for, it was more that we had respect for making a success of it all. At the Party in the Park, we played to 100,000 people. We were on stage for three minutes, and it felt like 30 seconds. We were at the top of our game and then, in early 2003, we got our second Brit Award, this time for Best Pop Act. That sealed it for me.

ANTONY

For me, success was when we turned up in the film *Love Actually*. Legendary rock star Billy Mack, played by one of my heroes, Bill Nighy, appeared on screen talking to Ant and Dec. There was a massive poster of a pop band behind him, and it was us! It felt very nice to be a part of cinematic history in one of the year's biggest films. As the story had it, we were meant to be Billy's competition for the Christmas number one, so he got out a magic marker pen and drew speech bubbles for us on the poster, writing in 'We've got little pricks'. Oh well, there's no such thing as bad publicity, I guess.

LEE

We could be a bit reckless. Okay, what I actually mean is, *I* could. I once walked through a hotel foyer and spotted a Christmas tree about 20 feet high. I'd love to say this happened at the Ritz in Paris or the Beverly Hills Polo Lounge, but actually it was the Hilton in Sheffield. So why did I feel the need to push it over, shouting 'Timber'? The same reason I poured tequila in a poor bloke's mouth in a bar while he was sleeping. Because it was there.

ANTONY

Growing up, I was often nipping into my local shopping centre, and every so often you'd see a famous person doing a signing at the Virgin Megastore. Then, one day, it was us. My brain always went backwards and forwards, remembering the past, dreaming of the future.

LEE

I think it's fair to say I was living very much for the here and now. I'd studied at the Italia Conti Academy of Theatre Arts, where one of that fine institution's most celebrated traditions had been taking part in fire extinguisher fights. With Blue, I felt duty-bound to extend this school sport further afield, and letting off extinguishers became one of my more popular party tricks, which endeared me to onlookers as much as you can imagine. Wherever we were appearing, I'd head straight for the bar afterwards and liberate the canisters.

On one ambitious occasion, I stood on a hotel balcony in Newcastle, gazing down at the fine diners on the restaurant terrace below. Of course, I was drunk. Of course, I sprayed them all from the fourth floor, being careful to put my finger over the nozzle for maximum impact. Down below, Alan Shearer got soaked. Dale Winton was running for cover. Security chased me, and I ended up paying for the entire clientele's dinner and drinks. The cost on that occasion: fair to high. The memory: priceless.

DUNCAN

We were flying somewhere literally every single day, and it was either helicopters or private jets, so it was full on all the time. We were glued together, but fortunately we never fell out with each other, we always got on. We were just young lads, earning money, travelling all over the globe, and having a complete laugh wherever we went. Not a care in the world.

LEE

Because we were always away, and this was the era before smartphones, the game Snake on our Nokias was our only form of accessible entertainment. We had only our wallets, our wits and our imaginations to keep us entertained, so we would banter with each other and start handing out dares to make the time pass more quickly. It was a recipe for, at best, easy distraction, at worst, disaster. Simon and Antony shared a room on tour because they were both a lot tidier than Duncan and me – they said our mess used to mess with their heads.

SIMON

When we were given our diary for the following month on a piece of paper, my first question was, 'When are the days off?' The answer was pretty much always, 'Oh sorry, fully booked at the moment. Something might drop off'. We had 14 days off the first year of being together.

For me, the only way to deal with that was to take each day as a surprise. When the car arrived each morning, I'd get in and ask, 'Where are we off to?' The answer was usually, 'Airport.' Then I'd wait to find out which country we were off to until we were in the departure lounge. The record company had it all under control – they'd done it loads of times before. And if I was ever really curious, I could just ask Antony.

ANTONY

Even when we weren't touring, our videos took us all over the place, as they became increasingly exotic. While we'd filmed 'All Rise' in Battersea Power Station, the video for 'One Love' was made in Los Angeles, in the same location as they'd filmed the car-racing scene in *Grease*. For 'You Make Me Wanna', we travelled to South Africa. The only way to process all those different experiences was to stay resolutely the same people in all situations, wherever we might happen to be.

LEE

For example, I took my fire extinguisher trick to the Far East. I used to like christening all the hotel doors with foam, as well as filling an unsuspecting hotel guest's shoes that he'd foolishly left in the hallway. On this trip, I accidentally picked up the wrong extinguisher, and next thing I knew orange smoke was filling the corridor. I ran into our room and persuaded the boys we needed to evacuate. We came into the foyer just as the hotel manager appeared. Deciding attack was the only form of defence, I started complaining like someone out of *Fawlty Towers*. To my eternal shame, this worked and he apologised profusely, but with a strange expression on his face. It was only when I went back to my room and looked in the bathroom mirror, I realised I was actually bright orange from head to toe.

ANTONY

On that same trip east, we were due to make a live appearance on Japanese breakfast TV. We were all sitting on the sofa smiling, ready to chat. Just as we were about to go on the air, we noticed Lee had nodded off.

LEE

Jet lag.

ANTONY

He'd come direct from a nightclub, he'd been up all night with two bottles of tequila for company, and was now snoring away. We put sunglasses and a hat on him and held him up between us. I had to be his ventriloquist – it was straight out of *Weekend at Bernie's*.

SIMON

It's impossible to grow up in those circumstances. Your every whim is indulged, every need satisfied. We had a fantastic tour manager, Johnny, who became our mum and dad in one person. All he asked of us was, 'Be on time, and be the best you can be on stage where you're serving the fans. Everything else is down to me.' And it was. Carrying the bags, calling a taxi, paying for the drinks . . . you name it. So much effort by so many people went into just making us look great, for starters. We'd turn up for work in our normal clothes, all messy and plain. Then the stylists would wave their magic wands and we'd appear in our ripped jeans, designer shirts, casual stubble, transformed into 'casually handsome' pop stars. You have no idea how many hundreds of hours' work went into keeping Duncan's fringe in its immaculate state! Everything you see on screen, on the front of magazine covers, it's all a mirage, the result of hours and hours of work. You're constantly being pampered like prize poodles, and after a while you don't even notice it's happening. It's a lovely life, but I'm amazed we didn't all turn into world-class divas with that kind of treatment.

LEE

Johnny kept us all relatively normal. Thank God he was there! I was a kid, so I relied on him totally.

DUNCAN

He fed us, watered us, kept us safe and went shopping when Lee ran out of underpants. We were completely and utterly protected. We didn't take the mickey, though. Johnny was too cool – he kept our feet on the ground when we could all too easily have lost our heads.

ANTONY

There was a wonderful moment in Dubai when we were all chilling by the pool in the afternoon. Lee couldn't get wet because he'd just had a tattoo done on his back, but the rest of us were mucking about in the water. Our dancers were in there as well, and Wham!'s 'Club Tropicana' came on the sound system. It was booming out, so I started doing his dance routine from the video. Next thing I knew, all our dancers, world-class professionals, had joined in behind me. There I was, a boy from Barnet, dancing in a swimming pool with a bunch of beautiful girls in bikinis following my every move. Who could ask for more?

SIMON

There was a dark side to that constant near-worship, though. One of the strangest things we noticed about life before and after the success of Blue was how people would laugh at things we said that weren't in the least bit funny. It began to dawn on us that perhaps this industry was built on quite shallow foundations. So we conducted experiments and started laughing to see who else laughed.

ANTONY

That was terrible. We'd say to one another, 'Who's going to tell a shit joke today?' and then we'd all fall about, waiting to see who else joined in.

SIMON

Noticing that all the time actually became a bit sad. But it made us tighter as a group, knowing we were all on the receiving end of the same treatment. We became like a family within a larger family, always on the inside, looking out.

ANTONY

And we never took the mickey. We never asked for blue dressing rooms, or blue M&Ms although we used to joke about it. The only things we needed were beer, vodka, rum . . . oh, and some hot water and lemon to look serious. We used to take the mickey out of those big American bands with their pre-concert bonding rituals. Our idea of a mantra was to put all our hands together at the start of every show and have everyone shout in unison, 'One, two, three . . . bollocks!' We're a sophisticated bunch, I tell you. That's a ritual that continues to this day. The one thing that stopped us all becoming stereotypical problem children was that we had one another to rein us in, to say, 'Don't be a dickhead'. So nobody was ever allowed to go too far – most of the time, anyway.

SIMON

In South Africa, Lee was on a jet ski, and the lifeguard said, 'Please don't jump in, there are dangerous fish and sharks in there.' So what does he do? He jumps in. And he says things are never his fault.

ANTONY

It hadn't occurred to me that anyone would be interested in writing about us as people, not when there were stars like David Beckham around. I thought it would be all about the music, but that proved to be very naïve.

SIMON

That was always the deal when we signed up, though. It was the era when tabloid showbiz columns were on the rise, and every entertainment reporter was looking to fill their page. If we didn't turn up in *The Sun*'s 'Bizarre', you could bet the *Mirror*'s 3AM Girls would have something to report about our latest exploits instead and with four single lads always out and about, we were low-hanging fruit to pick. We couldn't complain because all that coverage helped us get our name, and therefore our music, to fans who might never have heard of us otherwise. It was a win–win.

LEE

Our publicist, Simon Jones, who later went on to look after One Direction, always said as much. He told us openly that it was his job to keep us in the headlines. My mistake was thinking I could navigate it on my own terms. But then I wasn't the first, and I won't be the last young man to think he's controlling his destiny when all the evidence would indicate otherwise.

I probably did one or two cheeky things right at the start – for that is my way, you may not be surprised to hear – and suddenly, I was christened 'The Bad Boy of Blue' in all the papers. It takes a strong person to resist that kind of labelling, and I wasn't at all strong yet.

It didn't help that I've always had a problem with authority, ever since my school days, when I used to get upset with teachers and just walk out of my class. The fact is, I had dyslexia but it wasn't diagnosed then, so I just got labelled a troublemaker. At one point, they tried to force me to take the drug Ritalin for ADHD, but I refused. The teachers always told me I was going to end up in prison. I hated my school and I hated my headmaster and everything he stood for. I've always been a person to fight against the system.

Nor did it help that following the 9/11 debacle I had such a low opinion of the press. My manager kept trying to explain that the press could be my friend, but I didn't see it like that. To me, it was just one big conspiracy, so I thought behaving as badly as possible was a way of having the last laugh.

I'm not making excuses for my behaviour, just trying to explain why, when you're working out your own identity, it can be really hard when so many people, older and seemingly wiser than you, have their own preconceptions. You end up fulfilling their worst expectations. It's such a cliché, but because it's true. So I'd be interviewed all the time and I'd make up the most ridiculous stuff, just to see it turn up in print. I got known for it, so journalists couldn't wait to interview me, to hear the latest nonsense, then they'd go back to their editors and they'd print it. I was being used for headlines, but I didn't see it like that – I thought I was running the show. I thought, 'You're my vehicle to say whatever

I want, and you'll print it.' It was completely reckless of me, because it would be written up as though I was being serious, so readers quite understandably thought I was thick. I wasn't thick, I was just in the papers every single day, and I was a teenager so I'd long run out of anything important to say. One day I said I wanted to be Peter Pan, find my Wendy and have a baby. And they printed it.

The boys knew I had a good heart, and that anything they saw in print had probably been lost in translation somewhere along the way. Anyway, after 9/11, they were confident it could never be that bad again. I think our management lost patience, though, as dealing with it, and me, could be quite hard work. I remember being arrested for some fracas and phoning our manager at 5 o'clock in the morning. When he answered, before I even said 'Hello', he just asked, 'What have you done?'

He was right to enquire, as there was usually something. Like I said, you become the thing people believe you to be. In my case, on nights out it was the press telling me to 'Do something' so they could snap it for the next day's papers. With a couple of Jack Daniels inside me, I'd react – exactly what they were after. I'm not sure how much money I spent in fines for smashing people's cameras, and I'm not entirely sure why I thought I was still beating the system as I forked out the cash, and my name became increasingly mud. But live and learn, eh?

Fortunately, for the time I was in Blue at least, I was able to make up for it with the music. One day, I turned up with a steaming hangover for a recording session but also with a tune in my head. I met up with Antony, who'd been there since the crack of dawn, sat down in a corner for a couple of hours and wrote 'Breathe Easy', which became one of our biggest hits.

'THIS TEMPTATION'

ANTONY

I didn't know whether to be annoyed or impressed. Probably both.

LEE

The only time I'm ever really serious is when I'm in a studio, and I always wanted to improve the craft, so the first thing I bought with my new money was a home production system. Whatever mayhem I caused with fire extinguishers and Christmas trees, I always came back to the music, which probably kept me sane, and I could come up with the goods on the songs, which kept the label happy. Relatively. When one paycheque arrived, I walked into Harrods and bought a mini grand piano. It was Antony who asked me, 'What are you doing? You can't play.' 'I will,' I said — and I did.

CHAPTER 6

'INVITATION'

Mixing with the Greats

2002

DUNCAN

Friendships in show business are kind of accelerated because everyone's got cash to spend on having fun, and nobody has a desk in an office they have to be sitting at by 9 o'clock on Monday morning. Instead, you're always bumping into someone on the road, so you forge an intimacy really quickly, probably because you realise instinctively you're both leading quite an unusual life. For instance, I became friends with Jamie Oliver purely through both of us being on an aeroplane. We bumped into each other, had a chat, ended up going for dinner in New York, and next thing I knew, I was skiing with him on holiday. These friendships aren't necessarily shallow – and Jamie certainly isn't, he's lovely – but they definitely travel at their own velocity. And when you're flying high, you get a lot of offers and incredible invitations.

ANTONY

World-famous superstars crossed our paths like glamorous characters in a play. It's true that famous and semi-famous people become tethered together inside an invisible rope – mostly at airports, album launches, film premieres, anywhere champagne's being poured. The invites are endless, and we inevitably bumped into many of our idols we'd previously worshipped from afar.

Nobody let us down – everyone was amazing in their own way. It was a fantastic time to be a pop star. Blue moved as a pack of four wherever we went, so we always had partners in crime for any moments we might suddenly feel shy, which didn't happen very often.

SIMON

I always told the boys, 'Don't follow the party, let it come to you.' Whenever we were invited somewhere, we'd sit at a table and sure enough, within half an hour it was packed. People wanted to share our space. When we were together, something happened. It was strength in numbers, plus a bit of magic.

ANTONY

The Queen's jubilee concert, Party at the Palace, in 2002, gave us the chance to perform with two British music legends. When we walked into the rehearsal room in Bermondsey one morning, there was Phil Collins with his drumsticks. I was awestruck – I've always loved his music – until he came over and asked, 'Could you sign a CD for my daughter?' That was even before we got to sing with Phil 'Two Live Aids' Collins playing the bloody drums for us!

Later, we went to rehearse a number at AIR Studios in Hampstead with Sir Tom Jones. He wandered in, fat cigar on the go, and started on the routine. In my humble opinion, he didn't appear to be listening to the choreographer, and wasn't following the steps. We started getting worried . . . stupidly. Was Tiger Tom going to show us up on the night? Of course, *we* showed ourselves up by worrying about it. This was Sir Tom Jones, idiots! He knows when to turn it on. Sure enough, at the show there he was, up front and centre – every note, every move, perfect. Never doubt a legend.

After the concert, we were introduced to the Queen and even Lee could hardly speak, proving there is actually one person in the world with the power to shut him up. The Princes Harry and William were there too, really young, lots of white teeth, ever so well spoken, and they both said they liked our music. Bet they say that to all the boys! Like I said, it was a great time.

DUNCAN

I always loved going to LA, and I happened to be there during Oscar Week, which meant there were lots of parties going on, and I wangled an invitation to a private do, up in the Hollywood Hills. I was standing at the bar doing shots with Paris Hilton – as you do! – when I turned round and walked straight into Madonna. I thought she'd be an enormous, towering woman – as big as her image – but I realised I was looking down at her because, in real life, she's so small – perfectly proportioned, just little and incredibly cute. I said, 'Hello' and she replied, 'Heeyyy . . .' And that, I hate to say, was about it, because she stood smiling at me, but I found myself properly starstruck for one of the very few times in my life. I'm talking to Madonna . . . It was a proper pinch-me moment, and all I kept thinking was, 'I had no idea she'd be so little.'

Someone who did prove to be larger than life was Mariah Carey, and my exchanges with her got properly surreal. I didn't know her until one evening I was invited to have dinner with her at Claridge's in London, where she was staying. What did I tell you about strange friendships being forged out of nothing? Of course, I didn't know her already. Of course, I went along, propelled by flattery and curiosity, and there were a few other people there, too, but nobody who made an entrance quite like Ms Carey. I was standing with our marketing lady, Sara Freeman, at the bottom of the grand staircase in the foyer of the hotel when we spotted an eye-catching pair of legs up at the top. They appeared to be coming towards us – but sideways, not front onwards. It was like she was floating, not walking, in a tiny, glittery dress. I dragged my gaze upwards from those stunning pins, saw the body and finally the face of the legend that is Mariah. As a world-class diva, she did not disappoint. She looked me up and down and said, 'Heeyyy . . .' and suddenly I was floating too. I thought, 'I'm in love.'

It was a pleasant enough evening. She spoke to everyone and throughout the night would spot me and wave. I was properly intro-duced to her eventually, she thanked me for coming and that was it, off I went.

A few months later, I was flying from Los Angeles back to London, sitting in first class, waiting for the plane to take off, when we were told that we were being held up, waiting for one more passenger. Everyone was cursing the delay until this latecomer made her arrival and stopped all conversations in their tracks. I think we've learned by now that one thing Mariah Carey can do indisputably better than just about anyone else in the world is make an entrance. Sure enough, this dazzling vision in gold glided onto the plane, and was instantly forgiven for keeping everyone waiting. The same legs, the same thigh-skimming frock, the same massive sunglasses which, if I wasn't mistaken, had been discreetly lowered as she cast her gaze once again on yours truly.

I doubted she would remember me – how many people must she meet all over the world? – and settled back for a snooze until a few minutes later, her assistant arrived and uttered the pulse-quickening words, 'Miss Carey wonders if you would like to join her at the bar.' Seconds later, there I was, in Mariah's unique company and very much at her command, doing shots at 35,000 feet, and having her sing in my ear. Well, it passed the time. Could I call her a friend? Not in any true sense of the word. Could I invite her round to my house for a cup of tea? I wouldn't dare. Was I her chosen drinking partner for one night only? You betcha!

LEE

We once did a charity gig at 10 Downing Street. Cherie Blair turned up and stood talking to everyone, all friendly and smiling. I turned to her and asked, 'Would you like some chewing gum?' She said, 'Yes, please, I'd love some,' so I gave it to her. Except I hadn't mentioned it was trick chewing gum. I was always Dennis the Menace at school, ready with a stink bomb on the school bus, and this was no exception. Half an hour later, she came back, her mouth, her lips, even her teeth all bright blue. She said, ever so politely, 'Excuse me, did you give me some strongly coloured chewing gum?' Bless her, she didn't use the word 'trick'. Fortunately, she saw the funny side. It was a great antidote to the incident when my publicist nearly frogmarched me out after I'd refused to shake her husband's hand. Those two incidents with the Blairs could sum up the two sides of my personality throughout my entire life – the side that is angry, indignant, standing up for what I believe to be right, and the other side that is, quite frankly, ridiculous.

ANTONY

As I say, the entire course of my life has been influenced by my admiration for George Michael. He was everything that I admired, musically and personally, but although the band's path was crossing with those of many musical stars, it didn't occur to me to seek him out. Even at the height of Blue's fame, I knew our planets were travelling in different solar systems, or rather my little Pluto was orbiting around his Sun. Then, one day in 2004, Blue turned up to perform on *Top of the Pops* and we finished our dress rehearsal. The floor manager told us, 'Thanks, boys, you're done. It's George up next.' Everyone else wandered off, but I couldn't move. Sure enough, the man himself wandered in. I knew he was always very focused on his performances, so I didn't want to disturb him, but he walked up to me, 'Well, hello, if it isn't my fellow North London Greek boy.' I could hardly speak. He knew me! He carried on saying nice things – he liked Blue, knew our songs, spoke of a cousin of his who it turned out knew my family. Well, someone had to keep the conversation going, because I could hardly get my words out. It went by in a blur, but I'll always remember he said, 'Keep going, Antony. It's not always going to be this easy, but you can't give up. Not us Greeks, that's not what we do.'

Two years later, I was coming out of the LBC radio building when I saw a bunch of paparazzi waiting on the pavement. I started walking to the car before I heard, 'Hi Antony.' I turned round and it was George. This time I found my voice, and we had a quick chat. Then, in words I will treasure until my dying day, he told me, 'I appreciate all the nice things you say about me in interviews. We all have good times and bad times. Keep going.' And with that, he gave me a copy of his brand new CD single, 'An Easier Affair' – he said it was one of the very first prints, fresh that day – and he was off.

It's broken my heart that he's left us, but I'm so glad I had that moment, and I'm so glad I said all those things about him, and that he heard them. You should always tell people who you admire how you feel about them, because you never know.

SIMON

My musical idol was Michael Jackson and it was a suitably unusual encounter. It was 2006 in Bahrain when I was invited to dinner at a prince's palace, with the promise that I would get to meet Michael. 'Yeah, right,' I thought, but decided I would go along anyway, just on the off-chance . . . and there he was, standing in the hallway, saying 'Hi.' He was very, very gently spoken and when I shook his hand, it was bigger than mine but softer than anything I could possibly describe. I thought to myself, 'You've never opened a car door in your life.' The first thing that came into my head was '*Of Mice and Men*' and the bloke who kept stuffing his hands into a glove of Vaseline because he wanted to keep them soft. All of this was going on in the two minutes I was standing there, before we went into dinner.

This was Michael Jackson, so everybody was trying to talk to him, and I stood back. But, later, he turned to me and started the conversation with, 'How do you finish your songs?' I stared at him, wondering what advice I could possibly offer him, but he persisted, 'Do you write songs? How do you know when they're done?' I made a show of considering this for a moment, and then came up with this great nugget of musical know-how, 'You just know, I think.'

Michael considered this for a few moments, before nodding emphatically and saying, 'Yeah, I think I know what you mean.' Do you, creator of 'Beat It', 'Thriller', 'Billie Jean', 'The Man In The Mirror', my lifelong musical idol and uniquely talented superstar? Do you really? And we carried on eating. Like I said, bizarre.

Apart from Michael Jackson, I have no real idols in music the way the others do. Mine are more likely to be footballers, or boxers. Plus, I'm a Manchester United fan, so my biggest moment actually came later, after Blue had split, and I wanted to treat my daughter, Alanah, for her birthday. In 2006, I took her to meet Alex Ferguson and Wayne Rooney at Old Trafford, and even got to sneak into the inner sanctum of the team's changing room. Cristiano Ronaldo let out a big cheer and climbed out of his ice bath to say hello to me and a suitably overwhelmed Alanah. He had impeccable manners. I might not have played football professionally, but they knew who I was – for me it doesn't get better than that.

LEE

It does for me. In 2002, we'd almost finished our second album, *One Love*. It was just about ready to go to print when our record company boss, Hugh Goldsmith, suddenly announced, 'Something's missing, boys. I can see a duet happening.' Everybody else buggered off home, and Hugh asked me what songs I thought we could cover. I mentioned a few classics like 'Stuck On You' and 'Hello' before I got to 'Sorry Seems To Be The Hardest Word' by Elton John. It had been a hit, but it wasn't one of his biggest songs. That night, I went into the studio and recorded a version, just with piano, for Hugh to hear. Not only did he like it enough for it to go on the album, he said there and then, 'I'm phoning Elton's people.'

ANTONY

I was laughing. I told Lee, 'One, he's never going to know who we are. Two, he's not going to give us the song, and three, he's never going to duet with us.'

LEE

Next thing we knew, Elton had said he was a big fan of our music, he'd agreed to let us do the song, and had added that he'd play piano himself on the track. It was that swift, and that scary.

A few weeks later, he walked into the studio, in a tracksuit, and immediately lay down for a nap. He was tired from touring, but I was so chuffed, I wouldn't have cared if he'd just stayed snoozing on the sofa all afternoon. But he got up and played the piano for us, we sang and then he asked us, all casually, 'Do you mind if I put down a verse? Just to see how it sounds . . .' 'Do we *mind*?' I thought, 'we just got a duet with Elton John.'

I cannot possibly convey how much this meant to me. I got into drama school singing 'Your Song', although being a squeaky teenager I belted it out in a higher key than the one it was recorded in originally. Elton John was one of my biggest ever inspirations and ever since I was a small child, I'd told my mum how much I wished I could sing with him. She used to get me to go to bed by saying, 'If you pray hard enough and then go straight to sleep, it'll come true' and blow me if it didn't happen like that.

All sorts of things came out of that first meeting. After we released the song, Elton asked me to perform with him at a concert in South Africa, where I ended up sitting next to a sweet, smiley fellow, who then got up to speak to the audience. He became increasingly passionate as he told us that God was crying for us all, because his beautiful creation that was the world had been lost. His words brought tears to my own eyes and I whispered to the bloke on the other side of me, 'Who is that?' 'Archbishop Desmond Tutu,' he whispered back.

I visited an orphanage while I was there, which completely put all my so-called problems in perspective. We'd definitely entered another universe.

For me, though, the most memorable part of the whole thing was when Elton agreed to be in the video for 'Sorry Seems To Be The Hardest Word'. It wasn't something he normally did, and it came out of nowhere. We attended the Music Industry Trust Awards after we'd recorded the song, and Elton was there too, on another table. 'Go and ask him,' Simon told me. '*You* ask him,' I said to

Antony. Eventually, we sent Duncan over and the next thing we knew, we watched as Dunc bent down, literally on one bended knee, hands clasped in begging bowl mode, with Elton rubbing his chin, before he put us out of our misery and said he'd do it.

On the day of the video shoot, I remember just sitting, looking over at him at the piano and storing it up as a memory for the life-drawer. At the end of our version of the song, I'd added harmonies as Elton sang the main melody line. We'd already recorded our tracks separately, so the video would be the first time we actually sang together. As I stood up, I told myself, 'Just remember this. Whatever else you achieve in your life, always remember this moment, for when you need proof that dreams can come true.' I was just in awe of the man – still am.

ANTONY

Despite our stories from behind the VIP rope, you really don't meet the likes of Elton John every day, and I was dead impressed that Lee was able to sing as well as he did around him. I was so overwhelmed – I barely said two words the whole day.

I was similarly bashful around Stevie Wonder when we were given the chance to duet with him the following year. Unfortunately, on that occasion I did open my mouth, much to the horror of everyone around me. We were in a studio in LA, preparing to record 'Signed Sealed Delivered', and I suddenly noticed Stevie Wonder had quietly come in, and was patiently sitting by himself. Desperate to involve him, I took it upon myself to strike up a conversation. So I said the first thing that came into my head, as you do, which happened to be, 'Seen any good films lately?' Silence. Then, before he had a chance to answer, I kept digging – 'Would you like to come and see a film with us?' The boys just looked at me. Fortunately, Stevie Wonder proved what a class act he is, even when faced with a prize chump like yours truly. He just laughed and said, 'How about I drive you?'

DUNCAN

I should add that not every A-list encounter was quite so fortunate. One time, we were all very excited to receive an invitation from Donatella Versace to attend a fashion show in Milan as her personal guests, and then join her for an intimate soirée afterwards in one of her stunning palazzos. Apparently, she was a big fan of our music and had always wanted to meet us in person. Plane tickets arrived, front-row passes for the fashion show appeared, and things got even more glamorous when some stunning Versace outfits turned up that we were invited to wear on this pretty special occasion.

ANTONY

So off we went, all kitted out in the latest garb, flew to Milan where we sat on the front row of her fashion show. It was pretty boring, watching models walk up and down, so we got busy star-spotting familiar faces, like Lil' Kim. Afterwards, we lined up to meet Donatella, as though for the Queen, and put our hands out to shake hers as she approached. But she barely touched us, hardly looked at us and was gone in an instant. I said to Webby, 'That was a bit rude, I thought she said she liked us.'

DUNCAN

We were all a bit confused. There we were, dressed in her gear, VIP guests at her special party, and she couldn't wait to get away from us. We had no idea what we'd done.

ANTONY

It was only when we got back to London we discovered our boo-boo. Well, not really ours. A PR person had made a simple, but disastrous, error on the invitation. If we were confused, it turned out Donatella Versace was furious, thinking she'd been stood up by her favourite British band, after laying on plane tickets and all her best clothes for them. Apparently, she'd always been a massive fan of Blur and had been looking forward to meeting them. Whoops!

DUNCAN

Inevitably, behind the tales of glamour and incredible good luck, there were downsides to living such a hothouse existence. We were inside a bubble, and a lot of our connections to the real world got fractured.

I had a lot of old friends that I tried to make part of my new life, always inviting them along, picking up the bill, looking after them, trying not to let things get weird . . . But, of course, they *were* weird, because I overdid it. I didn't want my friends, who were struggling, to look down on me and think, 'Who does he think he is?' Instead, I just paid for everything. Gradually, I made a rod for my own back, with people taking me for granted, and getting funny with me. I'd always introduced everyone to the band, so the boys knew what was going on, and it would usually be one of them pointing out, 'You're being overly generous with people, and they're taking the mickey.' I heard it, but I didn't want to. Once I was travelling everywhere, it was easy for people to say I'd forgotten about them, that I didn't care. It culminated in old friends being lovely to my face, and putting the daggers in my back. Because I was an only child, my friends are like family to me, so it hurt me a lot. I learned the hard way that friendships shifted out of balance seldom remain straightforward.

ANTONY

My father used to tell me, if you can count the number of true friends on the fingers of one hand you're doing well. I didn't believe him then, but you do find out who your friends are.

Duncan moved around a lot growing up, so his friends were from all over the place, same with Lee and Webby, but I never moved that far, so my mates were ones from school, and they're the same ones to this day. My best friend, Andy Murray – not *that* one – never asked for a free ticket, not an autograph, nothing. He just wasn't interested, bless him. He was a manager at Woolworths, so one day it meant I was able to phone him up and say, 'Andy, we're coming to your store for a signing.' He replied, 'I know, mate – I've got the flippin' table set out in front of me. Had to move the pick'n'mix.' Completely unimpressed. Love that man! Twenty-five years of friendship. Same with my friend Tony . . . They were there when I was doing my dodgy pub gigs for £50 a week, they were there for Blue, and they were still there when I had nothing. Thick and thin, it means everything.

SIMON

My schoolfriends in Birmingham are real, and they're vocal about it. My friend Meetesh warned me when Blue happened, 'We'll drift apart.' I didn't believe him, but he was right; it was harder to see him, but I made it happen. I always felt, because of the fame and the associates around us every day, that I needed to be treated normally, and the only ones who would do that were my oldest friends. So I sought them out whenever I could, and heard the same welcome every time: 'Here's Webby.'

LEE

I found it really hard. Most of my mates were from working-class backgrounds like me, and it became difficult. I'd phone them up – 'What are you doing?' 'Nothing, what about you?' 'Oh, I've just finished recording with Elton John' or 'I've just been on stage with Tom Jones in front of the Queen'. It's really hard to avoid sounding like an absolute tosser. It became hard to relate to each other, and at that age, that's all you're looking for.

My family had always been a solid, grounding force for me, but all that travel meant I couldn't always see them. I remember ringing them up once from a five-star hotel in Japan, and hearing that everyone back home was dancing in the garden on a Sunday afternoon. I was having a lovely life on the road, but I ached to be back there.

I lost my way in so many ways, but I think that's an age-old story. It's just how it goes. I was still developing, I was always going to change and I can't blame myself for it now, but at the time it was quite confusing, working out exactly who to be.

CHAPTER 7

'TOO CLOSE'

Rumblings of Discontent

May 2005

ANTONY

We were in Italy. It was a beautiful town, and our stage had been built in the middle of the piazza. The setting couldn't have been more perfect, but behind the scenes, the cracks were definitely beginning to show. We'd just finished our soundcheck, ahead of the evening gig. I got something to eat and returned to what I thought was our dressing room. Except there was a bloke standing in front of our door, and he was blocking my way. 'Lee's really tired, he needs to rest his voice,' he told me. 'Well, that's our room. Where do you want me to go?' I asked him. He shrugged. 'Back to the canteen?'

DUNCAN

We never actually split. We never had a row, a discussion about going our separate ways, but things had just started to go a bit wayward over the previous six months or so. There was always the unspoken question regarding our relationship with the record company: What's going to happen after Blue? Who's going to do well, who won't? Who are they going to put their money on to make them more money? It's not going to last forever. Three UK number one albums in three years, 16 million records sold, number one records in more than 40 countries, two Brit Awards . . . Maybe that's our lot. When's it going to end, and what are we going to do?

The media played it up, naturally. We'd be sitting in the car together, all four of us happy, and then we'd see a newspaper headline, 'Are Blue about to split up?' We weren't, but it's almost as though if you say it enough times, you create it. The press created this tiny crack out of nothing, just for a story, and then it spread, just like a crack in the windscreen. You have to be very thick-skinned and well advised to withstand it. We were neither. And then, out of nowhere, Lee got a new manager.

ANTONY

We'd recorded the track with Stevie Wonder, 'Signed, Sealed, Delivered', which was great. But while we were working on it in Los Angeles, people from outside started to get involved with us – not me, but definitely the other three – whispering in their ears, 'You can do this, you can do that, you'd be great on your own, you should be thinking about solo stuff . . .' It was just a different vibe, and it didn't feel right.

DUNCAN

R&B star Angie Stone featured on 'Signed, Sealed, Delivered' along with Stevie Wonder, and it was through her that we were introduced to this unusual man called Jason. And, overnight, he became Lee's manager. Lee started having his own dressing room, while we sat there thinking, 'What on earth . . .?' This man kept telling Lee it was 'time to talk business', trying to get him on his own. When we turned up to gigs, we'd ask, 'Where's Lee?' 'He's in the dressing room next door.' 'Why?' 'That's what his manager asked for.' Okay . . .

Lee would say it was no big deal, they were just thinking about some offers, and none of us spoke much about it, because we didn't want to cause conflict, but it became really strange and caused an enormous divide.

SIMON

Lee told me some of the promises Jason and his team had made him – 'They're saying I should go and write with them, bruv' – and I was giving encouragement where I could, until Antony came and told me he feared Lee was being taken advantage of. I didn't want to see it myself, until we were in Italy, and that strange thing with the dressing room happened. Nobody was allowed in because Lee was 'warming up'. I thought, 'Fuck, fuck, fuck' – it was time to start thinking about myself, and I hated that, because up to that point, my whole existence had been linked to those three boys.

LEE

There was a reason for the dressing-room situation. When you're getting ready for a gig, warming up your voice, you don't want people coming in, laughing and joking. Antony's idea of a warm-up was a fag and a coffee. Those high notes were my responsibility and I had to work to get them. Antony just didn't like it because it was someone he didn't know hovering about outside. I've known him since I was 14, and if there's one thing that man hates, it's change.

But I was blind to the complexity of the situation, I know. If I'm honest, I should have seen it, but I didn't. Looking back, perhaps if there had been someone strong to pull me to one side and point it all out to me, I might have listened, I don't know. But that person didn't exist.

DUNCAN

We'd pretty much worked 20 hours a day, every single day, for four years without any breaks. We were travelling all over the world, spending almost every day in a different country, and everyone was getting tired. People were turning up late, and there wasn't the same energy as there had been. You could tell that people's hearts just weren't in it anymore.

LEE

I'd had enough, and I told the boys, 'I'm not doing this anymore, we've worked our arses off and we've got nothing to show for it.' Looking back, of course we all had loads more than we'd started out with, earned more than most people dream of, but having those big paycheques when you're too young to appreciate it can make you a bit blasé. Early on, following the success of 'All Rise', I splashed out on a brand new car before I'd even passed my driving test, which meant I got to look out of the window of a morning and admire my Porsche in the driveway, complete with L-plates. Lots of spending, much less thinking, did mean the bank accounts weren't as healthy as they could have been, and contributed to my frustration at that point.

For sure, there were people in my ear, starting to whisper, 'Why don't you leave? You can do better on your own.' But it was happening to all of us. Plus, our great mentor Hugh Goldsmith, who had been there at the beginning and who I had a lot of respect for, was leaving the record label. I could see it all crumbling, and I knew we'd struggle; it was on its way out.

SIMON

I thought we had more legs left in us, and it was a bit disappointing that there seemed to be an unspoken rift. You can't let whisperers in, because they'll always try to isolate you by saying you're the best one, carrying the others. We'd always said we wouldn't listen to that, but it got hard. It wasn't Lee himself who was causing it, it was the people around him. We didn't blame him, we blamed them.

DUNCAN

Lee was never going to resist someone telling him he was on track to be the next Justin Timberlake. Justin had become massive after leaving N'Sync, and this manager just blew similar-sounding smoke up every Lee Ryan orifice. Lee wasn't even paying him – the bloke just adored him and saw him as his next meal ticket.

But once Lee gets an idea in his head, that's it. Before you know it, he's off for a tarot reading. I think, on this occasion, it was the cards that told him it was all breaking down with the band. Over the years, Lee's kept us clued up on what the different cards mean, so when he told us The Tower had appeared – signifying sudden change, revelation, crisis, liberation, depending on what you read – we guessed it was curtains for us as a band. With all those voices already in his car, that was all he needed. I think, in the end, it was The Tower that did for Blue.

LEE

I had spoken to my mum's medium, and she had foreseen everything the way it turned out – my joining Blue, my leaving Blue and the solo projects that were coming my way. I know how it sounds, and I could be all conventional about it, making up something about creative differences, but the truth is, this is what actually happened. Going solo was the path I was on. I didn't know if it would be forever, I thought it might be more like an interval.

SIMON

The high-octane success we'd been experiencing was destined to come to an end, anyway. I didn't think it would be so abrupt, that certain radio stations would stop playing our records because they didn't appeal to a certain demographic. I thought that only happened to people like Status Quo and Cliff Richard. But there was a new kind of music supremo in town, and it wasn't one who had much time for boy and girl bands. My theory is that certain people in the industry had grown up when indie was all the rage in the mid-1990s, and now these same people were in positions of influence in the industry. If they thought boy and girl bands sounded too manufactured, not real enough, they were powerful enough to make them go away.

DUNCAN

Of course, the record label doesn't prepare you for any of this. They're busy trying to keep you in a happy bubble that they can control, with no mention of the reality that might come crashing down around you. They don't want you leaping before you're pushed, nor do they want you becoming too sure of yourselves, so that they can no longer control you while they still need you. I'm sure that's one of the reasons we were encouraged to travel so much, so that we didn't have time to sit down and take stock of our own value and where we might be headed. As we matured, however, we became four increasingly strong characters, a bunch of errant sheep desperately in need of a shepherd. If someone had been steering the ship, perhaps we could have altered our sound, thought about how to evolve together. Instead, with no one at the tiller, we started to run around in circles, making what we thought were wise, independent decisions, but without any understanding of where we were going.

We all started to be courted. Success comes with a lot of people blowing smoke up your arse – 'You can do anything' – and it definitely goes to your head.

I could understand what Lee was going through. My great love is musical theatre, so I was pretty overwhelmed myself when Andrew Lloyd Webber asked me to make a record for him ['I Believe My Heart']. He'd had a huge hit with Boyzone singing 'No Matter What' for his show, *Whistle Down the Wind*, so he was after the same crossover success for his new musical, *Woman in White*. I even got to make my own video, with this lovely girl called Keedie. The boys completely took the mickey – until it went to number one in the midweek chart, just pipped the following Sunday by Starley's 'Call On Me'.

ANTONY

I never had it in my head, but once I saw everyone else sorting themselves out, I thought I'd better get organised so I went out, knocked on some doors and got an acting agent. I didn't mention this, it just got added to all the other elephants in the room. Webby had a record deal and didn't speak of it, Duncan had signed a contract and didn't mention it, Lee was in the corner counting imaginary piles of money. . . Not a peep from anyone. 'What in God's name is going on here?' I thought. What hurt wasn't the evolution in the band, it was the lack of communication between us. I'd have said to any of them, 'Go for it,' and I'm sure they would have too, but no one wanted to talk. I didn't either, and I should have. It's the biggest regret I have, that I never confronted this issue, because I was a happy-go-lucky boy.

SIMON

I had some ideas about building a record label. I never wanted to be a manager, having to take the kind of calls at 3 o'clock in the morning that we used to make to our manager. But I was definitely interested in going into A&R, helping to influence the look and sound of an artist.

I was in a state of denial, though. I think there may have been a conversation about not making another album for a year, going on a break of some sort. I was in the room when it took place, but I wasn't really hearing it. 'You're not doing this to me,' I thought. My stakes were higher than for the other boys – I knew what it had taken for me to get out of Moss Side to start with, so that's why I think I felt the split so much harder than the rest of them. I never said anything at the time, mind you. I guess I'm saying it now.

Lee didn't see it, because it was all looking good for him. He does now. I believe you go through things for that reason, to learn the experience, and that was his journey: he needed to find out who he was, what was important, and he could only really do that by going solo. That boy got himself in such a muddle trying to keep everyone happy that it ended up being Daniel, our old manager, who sat him down and showed him what he needed to do, which was honour his commitments with Blue until the end of the tour, and then go his own way.

The fact was, Lee was having problems saying it, because he had too much respect for us, but equally our respect for him meant we had to open the door for him. If he'd just announced, 'I'm leaving,' we would never have got back together. It was the fact he felt bad that kept us bonded so tightly.

DUNCAN

For me, I had this extra burden during those latter years of Blue as I had this big gay secret: I was getting close to being outed, and I was becoming increasingly scared. I couldn't deal with being outed while I was in Blue – I didn't want to let the boys down, or the fans – and I thought it would be easier to deal with it on my own, and see it as a completely different chapter in my life. I was very frightened about what people would think, whether they would still like me, whether they would still want to work with me. It's silly, looking back, but these worries were huge in my head, weighing me down every day, and probably making me very difficult to live with. Even though I was frightened, it felt like a race against time, and I was sure I wanted to climb off the bus, this big Blue bus where I was sitting at the front, with a big pink banner above my head. I just wanted to jump off, before anybody noticed. I felt sure I'd be busted as, with the size of the Blue entourage, there was nowhere to hide. I couldn't cope with Lee's imminent departure either, and it felt like everything I'd known was falling apart. I just wandered around in a state of 'fuck, fuck, fuck', knowing I needed to jump ship for my own sanity, but having no idea how to go about it.

All this meant that I didn't cause the split, but I certainly didn't oppose it. Now I would definitely fight it, with the knowledge of what a small ripple my sexuality would prove to be. Back then, I was scared of the unknown, but I thought I'd take the leap of faith on my own, rather than bring the boys down with me. Finally, we had some sort of conversation between us and decided, 'Enough's enough. We need a break.'

We cobbled together a plan to take a month off, and asked our manager to pass on the message to our record company. Of course, they weren't best pleased, knowing far better than us that this was a sure sign the writing was on the wall. Instead, we pitched it as a holiday, pointing out we hadn't had any time off in four years. We did an interview, saying we were hoping to take a few months off, but there was no official plan for a sabbatical. When it came to it, we all just sat back as that hoped-for break turned into a year, then four years.

ANTONY

How did it actually end? We went off to Europe for the Best of Blue Tour, five months later than planned because Lee had hurt his throat, and finally got to Italy in July. We performed in some stunning locations, including the piazza in Lucca, in the northern part of the country. I should have been in my element, but Lee was already juggling Blue gigs with preparing for his solo album, and the others were equally distracted. One night while the rest of us partied, Lee disappeared for a photo shoot instead of leading the festivities, which I took as a sure sign of our world as we knew it turning upside down.

That infamous 'dressing room' tour behind us, we came back from Italy and that was it. No meeting. No announcement. Just . . . bosh. There was one last Wembley gig, where the setlist was pretty telling, with only half the songs actually by Blue. Lee sang one of his new solo tracks, so did Webby, and then Duncan popped up with his Andrew Lloyd Webber jazz hands. And I sang a cover. I've always enjoyed belting out 'Mustang Sally'. It was like karaoke night in Edgware all over again. But that wasn't even the beginning of the end, it was the end of the end.

Simon Jones had been running our publicity since 2002, and he'd done an amazing job for us. We always had a laugh and a joke, he said I'd never been late for him and we'd developed a good relation-ship – I thought. At a photo shoot just before the final tour, he came over and told me, 'You'd better find yourself new PR – I'm only taking Simon and Dunc. I'll be doing a bit of work with Lee, but I can't look after everyone, so I'm not going to be taking you on.' At the time it felt like a knife in the heart, it felt personal, even though it wasn't – he was just being professional. It's called show *business* for a reason, it's not show friends, however well we'd got on in the past. Besides, whatever I felt, there wasn't much I could do about it. In any other profession, you're lined up for a chat with your boss, or someone in HR to discuss your future prospects. Here, you're on your own. It's bonkers.

At the time I'd been going out with an actress in *Emmerdale* [Adele Silva, who played Kelly Windsor on the soap] for a couple of years, and when we got back from Italy, I went up to Leeds to stay with her. The following week, I was licking my wounds in a greasy spoon café when a bloke came up to me and said, 'Here, you used to be in that band, didn't you?' I replied, 'Yeah. What do you mean, *used to*?' He said, 'Well, you're not doing anything now, are you?' and I replied truthfully, 'I don't know, mate.'

He had a good point. I looked around the café, heard the tinkle of knives and forks, tea being poured into mugs and asked myself properly for the first time, 'What the fuck do I do now?'

CHAPTER 8

'MAKE IT HAPPEN'

Going It Alone – Duncan

Summer, 2005

DUNCAN

I really missed the boys as soon as we went our separate ways, but the thought of going back to Blue any time soon filled me with huge anxiety. I was stuck between a rock and a hard place. Plus, if I'm honest, I don't believe the amount of weed I'd smoked over the last decade was helping me in any way to sort my head out, either.

I should provide some context here. I think it's fair to say for much of the time at the height of Blue, I was stoned – day in, day out. It could be why both Lee and I have such problems remembering things these days. Antony always called himself 'the boring one', but it's probably why he could string a sentence together back then, and has such an undamaged mind to this day. His biggest weakness was vodka – but he'd have a couple and then it would be off to bed. That was usually when I was just lighting up another . . .

Mind you, he probably got high enough just from sitting in the car with us. He never said a word, just let us get on with it, unless I fell asleep just as we drawing up to a venue, and he'd have to shout,

113

'Dunc, Dunc, wake up.' Lee would be manically creative, crazily typing up scripts, writing songs, Simon would be listening to music on headphones, but I didn't do anything. I'd sit dreaming in my own little world, staring out of the window like a happy dog. It was like something out of *One Flew Over the Cuckoo's Nest*, but it worked for us.

Later, it was a way of dealing with the craziness. We had got so big, in places like Italy and Germany, where fans banged on car doors, that it felt scary. One girl nearly ripped my face – the boys laughed at me, 'Not the face' – and we would sit through signings where everyone just screamed. To cope with it all, Lee and I found the easiest way was to sit and smoke our way through a huge pile of weed. Everyone at the record company knew, but they were busy being equally young and cool.

When I hear tales of young bands now going off the rails, I completely understand that need for recklessness. Because everything else feels so out of your control, the temptation to retreat into your own little cannabis cave, where the world appears to slow down to a pace you can cope with, is overwhelming. It's wonderful meeting fans and saying hello, but it's also surprisingly tiring, and the rest of the day you're being shepherded to and fro. You start wondering how to take back a bit of control over your time. Before too long, Lee and I had extended our downtime pleasures into office hours, rolling joints on the way to signings, puffing on them furiously before they were taken away from us, putting on our sunglasses and sitting still for about three hours. Grinning widely in a thousand pictures, on the outside we looked deeply happy and engaged, on the inside we were high as kites. As long as we behaved, the record company didn't have a problem because it meant we weren't going to kick up a fuss about any aspect of their schedule, nor were we minded to while we were busy floating on this happy rainbow. It's a simple arrangement: fans go home happy, pictures in hand; we're great, they're great . . .

Love is all around. And now, more than a decade later, I'm left wondering how I would actually realise if I've got any brain damage.

Antony wasn't the only one who had to deal with us. One night in Frankfurt, it was my birthday, and we decided to head out for some revelry after a gig. Somebody in our crew had thought to mark my special day with the gift of some magic mushroom chocolate, which was very sweet. As he presented it to me, though, he kept saying, 'Just one square.' Well, within minutes, I'd had *two* squares and Lee had eaten the rest of the bar.

The next thing we knew, it hit us both like a truck and with fans everywhere, we decided the best thing to do would be to leg it out of the hotel. Trying desperately to find a spot where we wouldn't be recognised, we ended up on a roundabout in the middle of the main road, shrouded by some nice trees, just sitting and watching the world go by. This experience had all the components you can imagine — an epiphany about life, love, the universe and our place in it, an unzipped door into another portal, with inevitably a little cry by both of us as well. A proper, 100-carat mushroom-fuelled awakening, it felt like days we were sitting on that roundabout, although it was probably about 20 minutes.

As we walked back into the hotel foyer, who should we see but one of my great childhood pop idols, Susanna Hoffs of The Bangles fame? As you do. Somehow, my heart sent a message to my body, bypassing my brain, that the only appropriate thing to do on such an occasion was to let her know, very sincerely, how much her music had meant to me. I duly ran across the foyer, got down on my knees, literally, to break all of this to her . . . and I might also have mentioned taking some mushrooms. She stood patiently, seemingly listening to all of this, nervously looking around for security, and eventually, from the safety of the other side of the foyer with about 50 people between us, called out, 'Have fun, boys.' I've never met her since, and I would like to extend this official apology for scaring her in such a ridiculous, but well-meant fashion. She was a small but important part of one of the craziest, in some ways happiest, days of my life.

I felt the absolute opposite in the days immediately after the band split. My inner Redcoat got properly squashed, and I became very insular. People would come up to me, but I felt incapable of giving them anything. After all those years of travelling around, literally meeting and greeting so many new people every day, I felt depleted, running on empty for myself, so there was nothing spare to share with other people, whether they were fans just hoping for a picture, or good friends genuinely concerned and wanting to know what was going on with me.

My whole life, I'd always been able to deal with stuff, see the positive side of things and never had any issues with stress. Around this time, I started to struggle with sleep and anxiety, and it's something that's never fully gone away. At the time I saw smoking weed as an escape from my problems, the lure of staring at a blank wall, but in hindsight it really damaged me and may do for the rest of my life.

I was never a drinker, instead I smoked from the age of 16. I thought it was cool then, but I became very paranoid, and smoking to that extent caused me all sorts of issues of intense darkness, panic and sadness. The long-term consequences are still with me, and I feel as though my brain works a lot more slowly. There's no doubt it psychologically damages you.

If I hadn't smoked so much weed I don't think I would have needed to visit a psychiatrist and ended up on antidepressants around the time the band was splitting up. I might have been able to sit down with the people I most trusted and calmly work out what I was going to do with the opportunities I was being offered. Instead, I became terrified of heading out by myself into the big unknown, nursing my big gay secret, and generally stumbling into the next chapter of my life. I visited a doctor in Harley Street, and he put me on an antidepressant called Seroxat and ordered me to stop smoking weed immediately, as it was only fuelling my paranoia. He called Seroxat the 'Band-Aid over my wound, so it could heal', and started me on the smallest possible dosage. Two months later, I was on the highest dose imaginable, flying around on a magic carpet, thinking I'd sorted everything out. No more problems. If only . . .

Around that time I got a gig hosting the National Lottery on BBC One on Saturday nights. The pills were really working and I decided it was time for the Band-Aid to come off, so the doctor started to lower the dosage. I was also busy making a solo album, hosting lots of TV, being secretly gay, and I started to get terrible panic attacks. It would feel as though every time I moved my head, my vision would take a split second to follow, like feeling constantly seasick on a boat. The doctor told me it was a normal sensation for those patients weaning themselves off the pills.

So I carried on doing my stuff, and arrived at the BBC's Lottery HQ one evening to host the show. I was at the height of my panic attacks but, hey, there were only 5 million people watching. I started the show as usual and then − every presenter's nightmare − one of the machines with the balls in it broke down. This wouldn't be a big deal on your average quiz show, say, but there are all sorts of legal ramifications for the National Lottery, so it can never be accused of being fixed. We'd all been told what to say in such an emergency and I could see the autocue, but the words started spinning as the floor manager tried to find the right words for me. The script was swimming around, I couldn't hear anybody in my ear, the Lottery man with the big white gloves was busy with the machine, and I went into the worst panic I've ever had, live on air. What follows is arguably the most embarrassing incident of my entire professional life, and that includes being hypnotised on television, when I was convinced to fall in love with a mop disguised as Britney Spears, so I hope you're sufficiently prepared. Okay, here goes . . . I farted, and somehow − how to say it politely? − was unable to stop following through. So I stood there, a former boy-band-star-turned-primetime-TV-entertainer gazing out on the country's biggest audience, happily eating their dinners in front of the box. I could only think, 'Not only has the machine broken down, not only am I having a panic attack, not only am I secretly gay and taking antidepressants to cope with the stress of my band splitting up, but I have just soiled my underpants, live on air. Mr Duncan James, please take a bow.'

Somehow, I managed to say goodbye to the viewers, ran off the set, went straight to my dressing room, rang my agent and didn't even wait for him to speak. I just said, 'Never, ever book me on this gig again. I can't cope.'

The dictionary definition of the word 'humbling' is 'having a feeling of insignificance, inferiority, subservience', and that would seem to cover it, although I'm not sure it does justice entirely to the sentiments involved on that evening, or even the day after. It's an episode of my life I look back on and can now thankfully laugh at, but at the time it was horrendous. These days, whenever I have reason to return to that same studio and bump into any of the people in attendance on that stressful night, there's always an extra little smile exchanged as we silently salute the glamour of show business.

Fortunately, my panic attacks started to abate, coinciding with some offers of work on the London stage. Amazingly, I was given the choice of starring in either *Wicked* or *Chicago* in the West End. What a dilemma, two world-class productions! I picked the latter because the role of Billy Flynn in *Chicago* is so iconic. It all went off beautifully, we got great reviews and I was even invited to take the role to Broadway. But it didn't happen because at the same time I was offered a solo record deal, and I decided it was more important for me to stay in the UK, where I was already known. I didn't want to leave London as my stage profile was reaching such a critical point.

I never really wanted a solo musical career, I was the last person in the band to do it. Of the four of us, Simon had the greatest success, but I didn't like being on my own on the road. I was very happy presenting shows on TV, or appearing on stage, where there were teams around me, but I felt vulnerable and exposed up there on my own. I'm not cut out to be a solo artist. In my heart I've always been part of a band. When I did eventually get round to it, it was because the record company dangled a big fat cheque under my nose, and I thought, 'Fuck it.' But I went against what I really wanted to do, and just followed the money instead of my instincts. The result, the album *Future Past*, had some nice enough songs on it, but it was generally received with enthusiasm about as lukewarm as my efforts had been making it. What does 'Future Past' even mean? It was a lesson, hard but swiftly learnt.

Fortunately, another stage show came along: *Legally Blonde*. This seemed to be a bigger deal, with the co-starring role of Warner Huntington III one that lots of big names were after. The show's American producers came over to audition us, and they didn't care how famous anyone was already. Fortunately, I got the part and, with it, the chance to prove my real stage-performing chops. It was also where I found one of my closest friends to this day, the extraordinary Sheridan Smith. We started looking out for each other then, and have done ever since. She's also incredibly talented and gorgeous, and I'm so lucky to have my 'Babba' in my life.

While all this was going on for me, the boys and I stayed in touch, but it was clear we weren't as close as we had been, and that we didn't speak as much. It wasn't at all hostile, just busy, but it did feel weird in comparison with the previous few years when we'd been in each other's pockets. We just needed that space to grow. What was a testament to our friendship was how uncompetitive with each other we felt now we were all out there doing our own thing, how genuinely pleased everyone was when anybody got a good project under their belt.

Antony and I struggled the most, perhaps because we were striving in similar fields. We hardly spoke, and when we did, we seemed to brush each other up the wrong way. I think he found it tough going, and I should have tried harder, given him more attention, but I got busy – I feel bad about that now.

After his experience in the band, Antony felt he had more to prove. I was lucky, being offered presenting roles and shows. I think the assumption was, 'Duncan may not be the best, but he can do it well enough, and he can get some bums on seats.' With Antony, people didn't realise, but he could actually do it better than anybody. He's really talented on the theatrical side, but he wasn't the first call for some producers, and he took that quite personally. In this business you can't afford to get too down about any one opportunity lost along the way, you just have to keep going. I've known rejection and it stings, but I've always stayed positive – antidepressant era aside – thinking, 'Something will happen, I'll land on my feet.' Being an only child, I had no siblings to show me the way, or give me a leg-up in how to make it. Nor did I have anyone my own age at home to impress with my antics. This didn't make me lonely, it just made me realise very early on that if I wanted to entertain, or be entertained, I was going to have to get out there and do my thing. I started working full-time at the age of 16, so for me, it's always been a case of 'If in doubt, get out there and graft'.

CHAPTER 9

'BROKEN'

Going It Alone – Antony

2005

ANTONY

I was never going to be an amazing solo artist – I get that, I know where I fit. But my insecurities started in the studio. I was always the quiet one and I wasn't as naturally musical as the others, so I would tend to keep quiet. It was fine at first, we were all doing something we loved, but after a while it began to grate on me that I'd turned up first, been asked to sing loads of bits, and then when we heard it played back, I was only included in the chorus. I felt manipulated. I wanted to say, 'Tell me what you want. Do you want me to sing this bit or not? It doesn't matter, but if you don't, don't be crafty. Just tell me what you need and don't waste my time.'

Then, after we split, I went on *Never Mind The Buzzcocks* [in 2006, with Jeremy Clarkson presenting], and I was ready to have a laugh. I went on it knowing what to expect, realising I'd be the butt of jokes, but as the presenter got stuck in, I ran out of defences. He literally said, 'The other three are really talented, and Antony, you should just sit there, playing PlayStation.' I was laughing along, and then I got home and had a dark night of the soul, asking myself, 'Is that how people see me? Am I the useless one? The ugly one? The one that can't sing?' After a few hours of that, you decide it might well be true.

I know I'm different from the other boys. I'm a bit of a cockney geezer, my humour's blunt, and it can make me sound aggressive even when I'm just having a joke. Some of the producers, particularly the overseas ones, didn't always know how to take me, and in return, I thought they were often fake. Some 50-year-old white bloke would say to me, 'How's it going, bro?' and I'd think, 'Knob.' But they were all around us, these big fake American accents, and next thing I knew, the boys were speaking like that as well. I thought, 'Oh come on, behave.'

I spoke to Duncan about it, and he told me, quite rightly, 'We're all in it together, we all have to play a role.' So I thought about it. I was a cheeky chappy with my friends, and I remembered how performers like Robbie Williams had pulled that off on stage. So the next opportunity I got, I tried a bit of that, and then I got a message back from the record company, via one of the others, 'Oh, can you ask Antony to tone it down a little bit? He was too in your face with the crowd.' So then I tried sitting at the back, staying out of the way, and everyone started asking, 'Why are you so upset? Is everything all right at home? What's wrong with him? Has he got a bad attitude?' I couldn't win.

It was never the boys, it was the people around us that treated me differently. All the boys insisted that everyone be heard on the record, and they used to sing my praises, saying how organised I was, how they couldn't do it without me. But turning up on time, being the last to leave, I learned, doesn't mean anything in this business.

In Italy in 2003, Dolce & Gabbana gave us some clothes to do a photo shoot. They were really lovely suits and I couldn't wait for the magazine to come out and see the end product. I'd told my family all about it. Then when the issue came out, guess what? Not one picture of me, just of the other three. I think they included me in one photo with the band, but no big ones. Proper schoolyard hurtful stuff, it's an age-old problem. I was in a friendship group with three charismatic guys that were always the centre of attention wherever they went, and there's only so much love to go round. The fact that we were in a massive band selling millions of records didn't change the basic facts of life's lottery at the centre of it, and it's probably not very good for a young man just starting out, at that age when all you want to do is please people. It made me paranoid. I started looking at the record company, at the management, wondering, 'Where does this conspiracy start?' Then I even started looking at the boys, thinking, 'Have you lot been talking behind my back?' They hadn't, but it was in my head. I was 22 years old, in a group that was winning Brit Awards, selling millions of records, travelling all over the world and I was thinking, 'I've always wanted to be in a boy band, I'm doing what I love to do. Why do I constantly feel so shit?'

So that was my frame of mind when we finally threw in the towel after the Italian dressing room palaver. I assumed if there were any cakes to be had from the record company, they weren't exactly going to be coming my way on a platter. This fear was cemented the week after that final Wembley gig in July 2005, when I made a tentative call to the label. 'Hi, thought I'd phone for a chat,' I told an assistant. 'Sorry, this person's in a meeting.' No call back. I thought, 'Okay, you have your pride, give up now. That's the deal. You know where you stand. Get on with it, Costa.'

That fury, that indignation about being put to the bottom, was what kept me going through those first rough months. I kept thinking, 'I'm going to show the lot of you.' My family was gutted for me, but somehow we kept smiling.

The fury might have kept me on my feet, but my hunger to keep going and chase the so-called dream also had the unfortunate effect of propelling me into the waiting arms of all sorts of different people, promising, 'I can do this for you, I can do that'. I was so open to the next bright idea, I have to admit now I went against everything I believed in, because I just wanted to be out there in the spotlight still.

For example, not long after that dismal day in the greasy spoon, I met a producer who told me I could be the next Bruce Springsteen. Ridiculous! I had about as much chance of becoming the next Bruce Lee or Bruce Forsyth, but of course my ego was stroked and I went along with it. I had a family friend who worked in management, David Hahn, who kept telling me, 'Ant, these people aren't good for you,' but I ignored his advice.

In the autumn of 2005, my agent, Phil Dale, phoned to say he'd received a novel offer, for me to go into the jungle for that year's *I'm A Celebrity. . . Get Me Out of Here!* I thought it would be rubbish and everyone would take the mickey but I had a really friendly meeting at ITV with some very enthusiastic producers and decided to do it on behalf of Make a Wish Foundation. On the way to the studio where we were going to be introduced, I was in a cab and could hear a DJ on the radio discussing the line-up. 'Sheree Murphy . . . Jenny Frost . . . and we've got a has-been former pop star.' 'Blimey!' I thought. 'I've only been out of Blue for four months, give me a chance.'

Meanwhile, it seemed things were moving on the music front. Before I'd signed for the jungle, I'd been swayed by the dreams of a 'music manager' — that needs a LOT of inverted commas, by the way — and had already shot a video for a new single, 'Do You Ever Think Of Me?', a nice enough song but nothing spectacular. This man was convinced, or at least he convinced *me*, that I was on my way to mega solo stardom. The way he talked about it, I was going to be the next Peter Andre — all waterfall abs and a brand new career opening up. I wasn't fully convinced by the scale of the enterprise but I signed the contract, literally on top of a pizza box, the night before I was due to fly off to Australia, thinking 12 million people were about to see me on the telly and if even a fraction went out and bought the single, we'd be in business. I lasted two weeks in the jungle and this 'manager' was my first call when I came back across the bridge and returned to civilisation. 'Hi guys – what's happening?' 'Oh sorry, man, we haven't had the time.' Disaster. What a waste of time. The single, 'Do You Ever Think Of Me?', came out in February 2006 and didn't exactly hit the top spots. No surprises.

The jungle, however, was a revelation. I have to tell you, I loved it. It's such a cliché, but it was a turning point for me. I was finally somewhere I could be myself without being judged, which is pretty ironic, seeing as it was a reality TV show. A lot of people who take part in these programmes admit their wish is to show the audience what they're really like, and it's true. You don't know any of the other 11 contestants, so you can't prepare an act around them, you just have to be yourself and hope you get on. And this was a pretty random group of people by anyone's standards – Carol Thatcher, David Dickinson, Jilly Goolden, Cannon and Ball, Sid Owen, Sheree Murphy, Jenny Frost and Jimmy Osmond – but therein lies its charm. There's no nonsense, you just have to get on with it. Plus, you get so properly hungry in there, after a few days you really would do anything for some grub, and I did everything they threw at me. And it changed people's perceptions of me. Black cab drivers beeped their horns. Strangers came up to me on the street, saying, 'I hated you in the band, but now I think you're all right.' Bit of a backhanded compliment, that one, but I'll take it. I wouldn't say I reinvented myself, I'm not Madonna, but I certainly shed a skin in that Australian crocodile swamp.

The year 2006 was a funny old time. There was a bit of a false start, when I was persuaded to enter the contest for the UK's

Eurovision entry, where I was competing against people like Kym Marsh, but a man called Daz Simpson, singing a song called 'Teenage Life', won it. He ended up coming 19th in the main contest in Athens. By then, the rest of the Blue lads were all having success music-wise, and I decided it was time to find something I was good at. 'Lee's going solo, Dunc's going solo, Webby's going solo – what else is there?' I thought. And then I told myself, 'Well, I've sort of got my acting.'

A month later, I did two things on the same day that I'd never done before. I took all my clothes off for *Cosmopolitan* 'Nudes', and I auditioned for the West End stage. The nudity – tastefully done, I might add – was in aid of testicular cancer, and I jumped at the chance, because a friend of mine had suffered from it. I crossed paths with Ronan Keating on the way out of the door. He didn't look like it was something he did every day, either. We didn't say much, just tipped each other a knowing wink, both, I'm guessing, thinking the same thing – a pretty unusual gig, but a good cause close to both of our hearts.

In March 2006, my then girlfriend, Adele Silva, had a call from her agent, Alex McLean Williams, who knew I was a massive fan of the musical *Blood Brothers*. I don't know how she knew – I must have seriously gone on about it. I'd studied it at school for GCSE drama, and one afternoon our inspiring teacher, Mr Jones, had taken the whole class to the Phoenix Theatre, up in the West End, to see it. Now, Alex wanted to let me know they were holding auditions for the London production. My agent, Phil, didn't sound as enthusiastic when I told him. 'Eight shows a week – are you sure you're up to it?' he asked me. I had to persuade him just to let me go for the audition. I loved the show so much – I learned literally the whole script before I got to London.

There, waiting to meet me in St Mary's Church Hall in Paddington was the veteran producer Bill Kenwright. I was in awe of him, but it seemed it wasn't reciprocal. While he'd heard of the band, he clearly wasn't that impressed, and it turned out he was far more into his fifties and sixties rockers than any '00s pop. To him, I was just another face – which was the first time in 10 years that had happened to me. I was operating on neutral territory. The only thing he was wondering while he was looking at me was, 'Is this boy ready for the part?' I could hear some whispering going on around me – 'Why's he here? He's in a band, he's not an actor.'

'Time to show them, Costa,' I thought. So I launched into the passage I'd chosen, and he immediately put his hand up. 'I can't have messed this up already,' I thought. But he wanted to ask if I was from Liverpool, before saying, 'Good accent, okay, read on.' It was the biggest compliment I'd ever had. I've always been good with accents, and I'd been making an extra effort with this one, doing that thing all actors do to prepare for an important theatrical role, which is watching lots of *Brookside*. At the end of the monologue, Bill told me, 'I want to see you tomorrow.' Amazing! So I turned up, and that's when he said, 'I want you to start on Monday.' And that's how it happened. I was in the show for over a year, and it was both the best of times and worst of times.

The best? Well, it was the work itself, and I loved every single minute. At the stage door, people were waiting to talk to me, but for the first time in years, it wasn't about the band. They would say, 'You were great, I didn't realise you could sing.' Hang on a minute! Complimenting me to the point where I had to ask myself, 'Bloody hell, what have I been doing for five years in a band?' But hey, that's just the Eeyore in me.

It was a good time professionally, a new lease of life. I loved being the underdog, proving people wrong. Now I had room to breathe, and I was even working with people who arrived on time. 'Wow, this is what it's like when you're not the only one with a watch!' I realised.

From there it snowballed. The producer John Conway saw me in *Blood Brothers*, and gave me a part in the show *Boogie Nights*. I played in that for six months, with Alvin Stardust as my dad. Our dressing rooms were next to each other, and he used to regale me with tales of Marc Bolan and T. Rex. Then it was back to *Blood Brothers* – I do love that show.

One Wednesday afternoon matinee, I was doing Mickey Johnstone's big monologue, and I happened to glance out over the audience. I didn't usually catch people's eyes but for some reason that day I looked out, and I saw my old teacher, Mr Jones, sitting in one of the front rows with his class. I realised that I'd been one of those youngsters 12 years before. He smiled, and later left me a lovely note, saying, 'I always knew you'd be Mickey Johnstone.' I owe a lot to Mr Jones.

The worst of times? Sigh. For me the only blot on the horizon was a bloody great pound sign – or, more accurately, the complete lack thereof.

What can I tell you? Back in my school year book, I was once voted the pupil most likely to be the first to make a million pounds. I should go back and update that book to read, 'First to make a million pounds, first to lose it just as easily.' Elementary mistakes were made regarding the moneybags right from the first days of Blue. We were salaried employees back then, and the money was tightly controlled, but I spent whatever I had and didn't have the foresight to put away anything for tax. Like I said, elementary. I would say we were badly advised, but I know that's what everyone says and then it's time to reach for the world's smallest violin, so I might as well just give you the gruesome details . . .

I always wanted a massive house, and I got it back in 2003. At the time I was living in St Albans, but I thought Blue was going to last forever, and I thought I probably 'needed' a much bigger home. My dad, always pretty sharp, had advised me to put money into property. Being a wise egg, he probably had in mind something like student flats in Manchester, but I had other ideas. Then, one day, my mum watched a TV show called *Spend It Like Beckham* and she spotted a house that she loved in Hertfordshire. For a laugh, we said, 'Wonder if it's for sale' . . . and it was, which I decided was a sign. Next thing I knew, I had the keys. The mortgage wasn't exactly small – around £7,000 a month – but perfectly manageable while I was on tour with the boys, and I had a fabulous two years of partying there. Everyone used to come round, and every weekend I was the host with the most. It was like the wedding scene in *The Godfather* – or *My Big Fat Greek Wedding* in my case. Good times. I used to boast that I'd spent £52,000 on a telly. I could weep now at the money I used to drop on a single night – the sheer decadence of it.

Then, in 2005, the band split and, just like that, the money tap was turned off. Duncan was doing his music, Simon was doing his music, Lee was doing his music, and I was . . . shitting myself. Going into the jungle for *I'm a Celeb*. . . covered the mortgage for a few more months, but by the time I'd finished my first run in *Blood Brothers*, I was stuffed. Although I loved my newly found craft of theatre acting, it wasn't paying me enough to fund this massive house. So I tried to sell it, failed, and then the bank came and repossessed it instead in 2007. That was probably my lowest point, when I had to post the keys back and then sit down with my accountants a couple of weeks later. The house had gone, so I moved to Mill Hill and my new home, also known as my Uncle George's sofa. Oh, and then I had a phone call from the accountant, a pleasant enough chat in which we talked about the weather, caught up on our respective football teams and then he dropped casually into the conversation, 'You owe the taxman £600,000.' Oh yes!

I had thought everything was being sorted regarding all that, but the truth was, I couldn't buy a bus ticket. Everything had gone. As

I've mentioned before *Only Fools And Horses* was my all-time favourite TV show, and now, just like that, I'd turned into a real-life Derek Trotter. *This time next year, Rodney, we'll be . . . fucked.*

The depths to which I'd fallen were brought home to me in my accountant's office. We'd agreed I would enter an individual voluntary agreement, a way of getting the creditors off your back and paying the tax back as efficiently as you can, when my good man suddenly smiled and waved a big fat cheque in my face. 'Feeling rich?' he asked. 'Here's your latest royalty cheque.' It was for £69,000. And before I could even sniff a champagne cork, it went straight to the taxman. I literally watched as my financial fairy godfather put the cheque in the drawer, which he then slammed shut. I felt like a hungry Spaniel watching a big meaty bone being put back in the cupboard. Just about resisting the urge to dribble, I mustered up the energy to sign my name in the space provided. £69,000 – we're lucky to get 69 pence these days! Fortunately, it was just a piece of paper. I think I'd possibly be more gutted if I'd actually seen the cash and, anyway, it's only money. Aaaaaggghhh!

From then on my life became like that of a travelling minstrel. I was either on tour with a theatre company, or sleeping on my uncle's sofa. He always made sure I knew I had a base there and if it hadn't been for him, I may well have cracked up. I was only 25 at that point, but it felt like I'd already tasted more than my life's fair share of both success and humiliating failure. By then, I'd also become a father to a beautiful little girl called Emilie, born in 2004. Her mother was amazing, but at that time I was barely capable of looking after myself, let alone anyone else. It's my biggest regret from that period, and one I've tried to make up for in the years since.

It was very strange, having a famous face that people associated with wealth, glamour and success, and knowing myself that I barely had two coins to rub together. My response was to tuck myself away, spending time with few people save a couple of lifelong friends who had taken me on, literally for richer and for poorer as it turned out.

I stayed in touch with the other boys, but I couldn't talk to them about all of this. They had their own stuff going on, and anyway, I'm a proud Greek – I fight my own battles. I stayed in touch with everyone, the whole time I was flailing, and then as I started to put my pieces back together.

There was never any fallout between any of us, though. We were just doing our own thing, and we needed that space to breathe. There were always texts of 'Good luck, break a leg' whenever anything new came up. The respect and love were intact, despite what the press might have wished. They were desperate to drum up competition between us. 'Simon's record is doing really well – what are you up to?' A journalist would always try to catch me on the hop, hoping for a churlish response. Instead, I could say I was genuinely pleased for him, and I'd also sneak in a mention of my theatre work, which sometimes came as a surprise in the days before social media, which meant we could always get the word out. Oh well, a little bit of self-promotion never hurt.

As much as I loved the boys and how devastated I was when we split, it turned out I'd had to leave them to become the person I really wanted to be, through all the money problems as well as re-establishing myself professionally. Two things happen if you have to start again from the ground up. The first is that you literally have nowhere lower to go, and there is a bit of a relief that comes with that. The other is that, with every coin you put back in the piggy bank, comes another bit of self-respect, and that had been lacking in me for a long time.

I'd perceived all these problems about how I was valued, but the answer turned out to be more straightforward than I'd realised – get out there and graft.

CHAPTER 10

'SANCTUARY'

Going It Alone – Simon

Summer, 2005

SIMON

We decided to take a break, not really deliberate but unchallenged by anybody, for at least six months. There were phone calls here and there, but we definitely didn't see each other during that time. The first occasion we all got together deliberately was to go and see Antony on stage in *Blood Brothers*. And that came with an entourage – all our former dancers, our assistants, everybody. And then the group gradually got smaller on subsequent occasions, like university pals, work colleagues, every other friendship group in the world – we just had the press watching ours.

I felt really bad when any headlines came out, trying to compare us. Antony definitely got the brunt of that, he was unfairly picked on during our time in the band and afterwards. Journalists and radio DJs tried to outdo each other with their witty comments, and it chipped away at him until the armour fell off. During our time in the band, I kept reminding him, 'You're with three boys that love you.' Afterwards, it was even more simple: 'We've got your back.'

But we all had our turn. It was a choice of either be picked on or don't exist in the media's mind. But I was pretty philosophical about it all. There are always going to be people that don't like you, and they'll always want to voice their opinion. It's the price you pay for a public life, which is mostly great in so many other ways.

By the end of those first years of Blue, it had left its mark on me, though, and I was ready to walk away, pursue the Thai-boxing career I'd always dreamed of, or investigate going into MotoGP. Music had always been something of a diversion for me. However, it seemed my record company had other ideas, and I was offered a solo deal, so I ended up going down that road. It was strangely easy for me. They had an A&R exec. signed up, Jamie Nelson, who'd just worked with Kylie and had come over to their label, and he had an idea for the album. But he threw me by telling me, 'I'd like to have a discussion with you about which route you'd like to go.' What??? This had never happened before. With Blue, we always knew exactly what we were, and if we didn't, someone else had very strong ideas, but when you're asked for your own input, how do you decide? I was into rock, hip-hop, all sorts . . . In the end, it was *The Sun* newspaper that decided it for me. I read an article that announced, 'Simon Webbe is going to be the British answer to Usher.' I thought, 'Am I? Okay, I guess that's the box I'm in then. R&B it is.'

Left to my own devices, I'd rather have done rock music, along the lines of Lenny Kravitz and others, but I didn't think that would be sellable, and at the back of my mind, I thought the whole project was destined to fail, anyway, so at first I didn't want to put too much of myself into it. I'm always very statistical and I applied the same calculations to this as I do to everything: it's all about where you fit in. When Blue got together in the first place, it was because 5ive were splitting up and our record label had spotted a vacancy. Four years later, I looked at all the boy bands who went before us, saw who went solo, counted how many made it, and realised the odds were against me: Lee was our one. I thought I'd be the other guy, the 'one album and out' person. But that realisation brought about a change of attitude. I decided if it was only ever going to be one album that people heard by me, I'd better make it something that reflected my true roots and influences, and that brought me back to the music of my childhood. When I was really young, there was only one CD in the house, and that was by Bill Withers. I'd played it the whole time I was growing up. When asked to pen my first material, his song, 'Grandma's Hands', came into my head, so that inspired 'Lay Your Hands'. Then I played 'The Two Of Us' and that turned into my song, 'After All This Time'. I thought, 'This is going well.' So then I listened to his biggest hit, 'Lean On Me', which started, 'Sometimes in our life, we all have pain . . .' and I did my own version, which went, 'So, is this how it goes?' and that soon became 'No Worries'. In effect, my whole solo career came to fruition courtesy of Bill Withers – I hope he knows how grateful I am.

I recorded the album, *Sanctuary*, and it didn't sound like anything special in the studio, but when I heard it back, I was surprised. It didn't really sound like anybody else, and the whole thing turned out to be surprisingly successful.

How my material was presented to radio audiences really helped it succeed. Radio 1 asked listeners to tune in and try to guess who the voice behind 'Lay Your Hands' really was. People were phoning in to suggest names like Seal or even Prince, so when they learned it was me, they were surprised, and probably liked it more as a result. The album was released in November 2005, went to number seven in the UK chart and ended up going double platinum.

The second single, 'No Worries', changed my life in ways I hadn't predicted. As well as reaching the Top 10 in the UK in the same month, November 2005, it charted all over Europe, and I ended up being nominated for an MTV Asia Best Newcomer Award. When I got there, the other people shortlisted turned out to be Pussycat

Dolls, James Blunt and Kelly Clarkson, all massive sellers. It was like the Brits all over again. And then I won! So it really was like the Brits all over again.

More importantly, the song made its way to Thailand and found a place in the hearts of those citizens still picking themselves up after the devastating Boxing Day Tsunami of December 2004. They dubbed me 'The Healing Voice of Simon Webbe' and I was presented with a special award for the song's influence in lifting morale when the country needed it most. Then, during another trip to Asia, a woman came up to me and told me, 'Your song, "No Worries", helped me get over the death of my husband.' I'd always enjoyed music in all its different forms, but I'm not sure if I really registered how powerful it could be until then. Here I was, the quiet one from Blue who no one really knew about, and yet something I'd created could have this effect on people, something important. My mum used to say, 'There is no such thing as a selfless deed' and I didn't believe her, but the satisfaction I got from hearing that nice lady's words to me about what my song had done, well, now I believe my mum. Never have I been more proud. It was a song I'd actually forgotten I'd recorded, and it turned out to be the most important thing I ever did on my own.

Other good things happened along the way. I'm a big Marvel fan and I got to record a track ['Ride The Storm', a double A-side with the single 'Grace'] for the *Fantastic Four* sequel soundtrack, *Rise of the Silver Surfer*, so that's something to tell the grandchildren. But despite this, my solo success began to wane. If I was being analytical, I could say that I was a victim of my own success. The first album, *Sanctuary*, had been budgeted to sell around 30,000 copies, so when it sold a whopping 700,000 instead and was certified double platinum, the label decided not to release any more singles, but to press on and release my second album, *Grace,* in November 2006. To my mind, it was released too close to the first one and listeners got confused, not realising there was new music available. It might have had a life of its own if released later, but probably needed a bit more coal in the engine of publicity. Either way, it sold less than half the amount of the previous one, and I was no longer the record label's golden child.

I took that in my stride – I wasn't going to sit there with a chip on my shoulder, watching someone else have a go. The whole pop music industry is designed like any other business, to embrace new sounds and voices, and clear out the old. It rotates like a wheel, and, like many other people before me, I was the hamster: you have to find a place within it where you feel relevant, or jump off. Either way, the wheel will continue to turn. I wasn't sure where I fitted in, and instead I thought, 'I think I'll just leave it. I've had two great albums, let's not jinx it.'

The truth of the matter was I missed being in a band. The first time I performed 'Lay Your Hands' live, I sang the first verse and then put my microphone down for someone else to sing. But there was no one there. I stood there, thinking, 'Where is everyone? Oh shit, it's just me!'

As it happened, on the promo circuit that year I bizarrely often had Lee for company, as he was doing the same rounds with his music, so we kept bumping into each other, which made it fun, but also in some ways highlighted my loneliness the rest of the time.

I've never really had any self-belief when it comes to music. I'd been perfectly happy hiding behind the boys, doing my own little thing, happy to be there. Whatever I've turned my hand to has always been motivated by the pursuit of approval from others. I grew up with just my mum, and she was strict. She made it clear, 'I'm not your friend, I'm your mother.' She's an amazing woman, full of self-respect, her own morals and set of values – even when I made enough money to buy her a house, she stayed where she was and stuck to her roots – but she was a single parent with a strong hand, so any praise I went after had to come from outside the home. I always sought out older people – teachers, friends, anybody – and then set about getting their approval. At school, I was naturally quick at sports, always kicking a ball. The first game of football I ever played, I scored five goals. Everyone shouted and jumped on me, and I thought, 'Wow, this is nice.' Whatever I've done since – music, acting, meeting fans – I've basically been chasing that same feeling – undiluted praise and approval – since I was nine years old.

Meanwhile, as is the passage of former pop stars, I had my pick of offers when it came to reality TV. I turned a lot down that I didn't think were really me – for example, the invitations to go on dating shows when I already had a girlfriend. 'Just come on anyway, it'll be fun,' they said. 'Fun for who?' I wondered. However, when I was invited into the celebrity jungle myself in 2008, it only took one call to Mr Antony Costa to persuade me. I wanted to challenge myself and, because I'm terrified of water and spiders, this seemed like the perfect opportunity. Antony encouraged me by saying it was the best thing he'd ever done, but he didn't really tell me the full story – the long days, the hunger, the boredom. I was with a nice enough bunch of people – Joe Swash, George Takei, Dani Behr, Martina Navratilova, Robert Kilroy-Silk, Timmy Mallett, Esther Rantzen, David Van Day and Brian Paddick – but by the end of the first day, I was aching to go home. I even asked if I could, but the producers let me know that if I left, my chosen charity, ACLT (African-Caribbean Leukaemia Trust), wouldn't get any money. So I stayed put, but I found it almost intolerable. The worst part was waking up in the morning, and finding a camera right in my face. I'd thought I'd be incredibly chilled with everyone the whole time I was in there, but as the days went by, I found myself getting caught up in silly spats. I'd become friends with some of the girls, and ended up being their protector, which caused some aggro. Plus, you don't realise how you're coming across on TV. One evening, former Dollar star, David Van Day, told me he was going to take my bed and said I could sleep in the cave. 'If you don't leave me alone, I'll throw *you* in the cave!' I replied. I was just having a laugh, but on the screen and in people's living rooms that came across as really hostile and aggressive. I realise now how these things can take on a life of their own.

Despite my reluctance, I did well in the jungle and ended up reaching the semi-finals, staying in there for 19 days. The press were great, and as soon as I returned home to the UK, different offers started arriving. One I wasn't able to resist was the prospect of appearing in *Sister Act* on the London stage, alongside Whoopi Goldberg and Sheila Hancock. In such world-class company even the rehearsals were nerve-wracking. I felt like I was auditioning for my supper all over again. When I got up on stage for the first time with Sheila Hancock, it was as though her piercing blue eyes were staring straight into my soul, and I thought, 'Blimey, this acting business is really intense.' It was only when I was sharing a cup of tea with her afterwards I realised that her eyes were always like that, just stunning. And Whoopi played games with us all on stage, trying to throw us off our stride, keeping it alive and interesting. She wanted to help me, asking me for suggestions as to how I thought I should say my lines. Eventually, I told her, 'You're the Oscar winner, you tell me.' They became like another family for four months.

Looking back, I don't think I began to evolve in any meaningful, adult way until the band split, and I was forced to. Being in that bubble of fun was great, fans running after the van and everything else involved. While you're experiencing it at a young age, it's very hard to imagine it'll ever stop and be something in the past. Then, when it does, it comes as a sharp shock to realise you have no identity of your own and that you're actually at a bit of a disadvantage to the people around you. So many things were done for us – car doors opened, passports checked, suitcases carried – that we simply had no idea how to operate when we were thrown back into the real world. I had to relearn how to go on holiday by myself, how to turn up to the right airport terminal and all that stuff, just as I was about to turn thirty. How embarrassing. But there's no alternative, no way of turning back the clock and nowhere to hide. You just have to start working on it and making up for lost time.

CHAPTER 11

'I AM WHO I AM'

Going It Alone – Lee

2005

LEE

I was the chosen one, was I? The golden egg? Well, what can I tell you? The gods had other plans. I was courted by top managers, producers, record labels . . . I got a solo deal with Sony BMG and, guess what? I ended up hating it. As soon as I was signed, it was clear the record company and I had very different ideas about what kind of music I should be making. I was young and naïve, and had no idea about the business, about the way things work. I wanted to do soul music, but my new bosses instead opened the pages of *Music Week* in 2005, saw indie, indie, indie, and told me, 'You're making an indie album.' They suggested I look at the Top 10, and see where the future was headed. 'Shit,' I thought.

I spent ages trying to persuade them that there was a gap for a soul album, that they were just following trends and that there was other music to be had. But this was long before Amy Winehouse or James Morrison turned up, and they were more interested in the likes of Maroon 5. Basically, we didn't see eye to eye, and I was told what to do. One exec. rang me up, telling me to record some terrible song about a stripper. When I refused, he shouted, 'This isn't Blue anymore. This is you on your own and you will do what the fuck I tell you to do.'

Ho-hum. It took three weeks to record *Lee Ryan*, the album, although it felt a lot longer. Don't get me wrong, it did have some good songs on it – In July 2005 'Army of Lovers' got to number three in the UK charts, and reached number one in our old stomping ground of Italy.

'Turn Your Car Around' would be a really good song to sing now I'm older, but it was a bit middle of the road for that time in my life, bearing in mind I was meant to be carrying with me a massive teenage fan base over from Blue. 'Real Love' was fun, and turned up on the soundtrack of the animation film, *Ice Age: The Meltdown*. That was a funny story, actually; my involvement with the music led to my meeting the dubbing guys from the film, which led to my being cast as – are you ready for this? – an elk in the British version of the film. I'm guessing that would be a spear-carrier in human terms. It got even better with the Italian version, where I was asked to voice one of the main characters, Eddie . . . in Italian. Somehow I carried that off, and I've turned up in the three later films in the series, all in Italian. And you thought *EastEnders* was a fluke?

Elk duties aside, that whole chapter in my so-called solo career was okay, but it really wasn't me, it didn't touch my roots at all, and I'm sure the people who listened to it could tell. The album got into the Top 10, but if I'm honest, it felt like this new era in my life was dying on its arse before it had really begun. I started working on the second album, but that got even more depressing. The record label wanted one thing, my manager another. We released a charity single – 'Reinforce Love' – and when that failed spectacularly to find an audience, everyone started second-guessing themselves. One typical afternoon, I had a meeting with one record exec. who announced confidently enough, 'What we want from you is straight pop, no licks, no soul, just give me a pop song.' An hour later, I received a phone call from his fellow exec., saying, 'We've worked it out. We want George Michael, Elton John, something really soulful.' I felt like knocking their heads together. 'Who should I listen to?' I asked. 'I don't know,' was the answer. 'Can you ring my manager?' 'I can't do that, I don't want to upset him.'

You'll be amazed to learn the album never got off the ground. The one thing they were agreed on is that it was probably my fault, particularly when I started speaking even more strongly about the kind of music I wanted to work on. Or 'being trouble' as they put it. Looking back, perhaps a nine-minute song about Jesus's life wasn't exactly what they were after. For another song, 'Time Flies', I spent the money myself, the best part of £20,000 on an orchestra. Then there was another one called 'Indian Song' which I planned to invite a Native American to perform on. Perhaps it did get a little ambitious, but I always say, if you have a vision . . .

I was pretty downbeat about the whole thing, and that was before I went to perform at a gig, and was booed off stage, people literally chucking bottles at me. 'That's it, I can't be in this country anymore,' I thought. 'I have to leave before it destroys me. I'm turning into someone I don't want to be.' It was pretty brutal, and that's what prompted me to move to America.

It had always been my teenage dream to go and live in California. It's what I'd always planned before Blue turned up in my life. By the time I got there, I hadn't exactly been living the dream, at least not their healthy, sea-air version of it. I was overweight, I'd been taking too many drugs and drinking too much, so I wasn't feeling great, but the fabled LA lifestyle helped get me back on track. I still had a bit of money in my back pocket, so I found an apartment on Venice Beach, only a few steps from the Pacific Ocean, started running and just hanging out in the sunshine. I made some obligatory rounds of agents, both musical and acting, and some gave me the spiel they gave everyone else, tapping their cigars and telling me they were going to make me a star, but I wasn't actually too bothered at that point – I was pretty happy just enjoying normality again. I was 23, sitting on the beach, and I thought it might well be time to retire.

I actually went to America to forget who I was. It was the first time in years I'd had a chance to go away and make friends on the merit of me, not of being in Blue, and that was an eye-opening experience, for good and for bad. But I found some peace in myself, and it hopefully made me a better person.

I was in America for two years. I could have stayed there longer, but, as is the age-old tale, I met a nice girl and she started making noises about settling down somewhere together, even putting a ring on it. That prompted some soul-searching on my part: Is my creative life behind me? What will I do? And do I want to get married? The answers were: Hopefully no, not sure and definitely not. I worked out it was time to come home, even if I wasn't sure what the future looked like.

Music was still my first calling, but it seemed as though every time I tried to get back into the industry in some meaningful way, it went wrong. This became evident a few years later, when working once again on my second solo album made me feel even more downhearted. Despite my years in the business, I still felt like a puppet working for men in suits and, as soon as that puppet stopped dancing to their tune, whatever they decided it was going to be on that particular day of the week, they cut the strings. Just like that. Dropped like a stone. But what can you do? There was one beautiful song on that aborted second album, 'I Am Who I Am', which I'll always be proud of but, that aside, both times I've tried, my solo projects have been pretty disastrous. I'm clearly not meant to go it alone.

During the time I was living in America, I started being offered stints on British reality TV shows. It all seemed straightforward enough at the time. I wouldn't say I enjoyed appearing on that kind of show, I saw it more as a means to an end. My plan was to make some money, and then take it back with me to the US, where it would go so much further – back then, anyway.

Even though the plan was always to keep my head down, keep smiling, take the money and run, I never quite had the self-control to dodge the brickbats when they came flying out of nowhere. I'd got better at responding, not reacting, if I knew what was coming, but the surprises continued to catch me out. So it was with a light heart that in September 2007, I signed up for *Hell's Kitchen* in the UK. What could go wrong? I love cooking.

I was teamed up with your usual random assortment of reality TV people. Where else would you have Anneka Rice, Barry McGuigan, Abbey Clancy and Jim Davidson all in the same room, let alone all wearing chef's whites? It was the third series, and the original head chef, Gordon Ramsay, who I knew I could get on with, had been replaced by Marco Pierre White, a bit more of an unknown quantity. Very soon, it was clear that Marco didn't take it well when the judges criticised the dishes he'd put together, and he tried to lay the blame for the food on the contestants, even though he was responsible for the combinations. On the first night, he used the phrase 'pikeys' picnic' to talk about the food, which I found a really disparaging way of referring to the traveller community. The first time I kept my mouth shut, but when he repeated it, I decided I had to say something. I have friends from the traveller community, and they find it a really derogatory term so I wasn't prepared to sit back and let someone speak like that in front of me, however much money I was being paid. Like I said, I could be hot-tempered but I've never been a hypocrite. So I went and asked him not to use the phrase, live on camera, and he turned on me. I kept my temper, but he started speaking really slowly, like a Bond villain, and it was clear my card was marked. He even said, 'Be very careful. I will deal with you in my own time, you'll see.' Hilarious. So we ended up having a blazing row, and he told me, 'Go back to your living quarters.'

I went outside for a breather and when I came back in, he told me I was off the team. 'Do you want me off the show?' I asked and he said, 'Yes.' They edited that bit out, of course, so it looked like I stormed off, but I didn't, he kicked me off. What I found a bit odd when I watched it back was hearing him say he would have been happy to discuss it if I hadn't been 'so aggressive'. Aggressive? You can see me cowering as I asked to speak to him. I was trembling like a schoolboy waiting to see the headmaster.

Despite Marco's fury at the time, a lot of good came out of that spat. For a long time after the show aired, with me pulling my little suitcase on wheels out of the kitchen after three short days, I had a lot of people from the Romany community approach me to say thank you for sticking up for them.

Unsurprisingly, with that kind of thing going on, it didn't take me long to really dislike appearing on TV reality shows. I just felt like a performing monkey every time. In fact, soon after *Hell's Kitchen*, I vowed I'd never do another one. If only I'd remembered that promise to myself when the phone rang in 2012, inviting me on to *Celebrity Big Brother*. Oh well . . .

The press always delighted in the fact that I met the mother of my son on Myspace. Somewhere it was reported by 'a close friend' that she was a lifelong fan of the band, that she'd sent me naked pictures of herself via the then-hot website, and that as soon as I saw them, I contacted her. That story got repeated so often, it became accepted as fact, and no amount of denying made any difference. Don't let the truth get in the way of a good story, I say.

Well, sorry, folks, but even I'm not THAT shallow, and Sami, the lady in question, definitely isn't either. The truth is, she didn't send me any saucy pictures, and she wasn't even a fan of the band. There was no 'If I sign your T-shirt, will you take it off?' chat or any of that business. During my time in America, Sami had sent me a message via the website, and we became – get this – pen pals. Remember them? We chatted for a year and a half by email before we first met. I remember everyone taking the mickey out of me for meeting somebody online, and now the whole world does it. She wasn't a fan of the band at all, she delighted in telling me she preferred Nirvana, but we just got on. We chatted by email for all those months, and it was only when I returned to the UK to take part in *Hell's Kitchen* that we finally met up in person, and the rest is history.

We laughed about the press getting it so wrong, but it didn't help that there were so many daggers out there, waiting to cause damage wherever they could. It was the downside to having such a public profile. Because Blue had long split up by the time we met, Sami wasn't really prepared for how famous our faces still were, how much attention we all got everywhere we went, and that caused a lot of stress in our relationship. Our son, Rain, came along in November 2008, and we both fell completely in love with him, but even then, we couldn't escape rumours about the state of our relationship. A story appeared that, immediately after he was born, I'd walked out on both of them. It came out of nowhere but caused me all sorts of problems, with everyone slagging me off in the press and even family members reading it and believing the story until I was able to convince them otherwise.

Meanwhile, we were a young couple making all the same mistakes every young couple makes, except every time we fell out, the papers were all over us, which of course added more stress to an already turbulent relationship. It became a vicious circle, and the cracks began to show. The bottle has always been my refuge of choice and I began disappearing into it. What should have been one of the happiest times in my life because of the arrival of our son instead became really difficult. I often lost my temper, much to the press's delight. There's one abiding image of me flinging money at Sami in the street that I'll always regret, but what the accompanying stories all failed to include was that we'd made up long before the ink on those pages had dried. But it all got too much for both of us, and eventually, after many tearful break-ups and make-ups over six years, Sami and I had to finally go our separate ways. The day we split up was one of the saddest days of my life, but somehow even then we were able to make our son our priority. It hasn't always been straightforward, but thankfully now we are great friends with the past firmly behind us. I wouldn't be the man I am today, which is hopefully a better one, without the lessons I learned in our relationship. We have our wonderful son, so we'll be in each other's lives forever. We both love him and she's a great mum, so we'll work it out.

I'm not sure I'm the settling-down type, to be honest. There have been many beautiful women in my life, but there have only been one or two since I first joined Blue that haven't gone on to sell stories on me, which could be why I've become a bit of a commit-ment phobe. Or, to be fair to them, it could just be the other way round. Hmmm . . . But there does seem to be a bit of a similar theme to all of my romances. I'll meet a lovely girl, I'll tell her how it's happened a lot, she'll say, 'I'm not like that, I'd never do that' . . . and then she does! So I don't like to open up these days. I'm not sure I want a relationship badly enough. My son Rain and my daughter Blubelle will forever be my priorities, and my favourite time is always the time I spend with them.

Otherwise there's always something creative I want to be getting on with. I used to have a lovely flat by the Thames, where I'd created some of my own art on the walls, and I enjoyed working on it late into the night. One evening, my then girlfriend kept trying to distract me, and eventually went off to bed by herself. The next morning, I woke up and she'd disappeared, leaving a pretty direct message on the wall. She'd written in black marker pen, 'You may love to draw, but your drawings will never love you.' Whoops! It took me ages to clean that off.

So, relationships and me . . . In a nutshell, I'm no good at them. I'm a bit of a dreamer, and the hopeless romantic in me always thinks someone else might walk in and the violins will start playing. I mean, they always do for a while, but, if I'm truthful, I'm holding out for the full symphony . . .

CHAPTER 12

'SORRY SEEMS TO BE THE HARDEST WORD'

Duncan's Struggles With His Sexuality

2009

DUNCAN

I'm not a confident person. Anything you might mistake for confidence or self-belief is actually just a performer's trick. All my life, I've always had a lot of insecurities and self-doubt – people tell me it's the same with many people who choose to go into the entertainment business. As an only child desperate to make friends, I relied on my charm growing up, and then, when I got into a band, that turned into showmanship. Suddenly I was Duncan from Blue, and I knew exactly what was required of that person. A lot of people used to think I was very arrogant, overly confident and sure of myself. The opposite was actually true, but I was always able to get up and switch it on when required – smiling, joking, not a care in the world. It didn't mean that when the cameras stopped rolling and the lights went off, that's who I really was – in fact, it was the opposite.

The first few years of Blue made it easy to perfect that persona. It was all fun and exciting, with people recognising us but not really asking too much of us. We were inside that bubble, completely protected and not having to ask too many questions of ourselves. Outside the bubble, the press took one look at my floppy hair, my big blue eyes, my constant smile to camera, and within weeks of Blue appearing on the scene had me tagged a 'ladies' man'. That really was all it took, and of course I played along.

Before I even became a familiar face with Blue and was invited to events crowded from wall to wall with A-list glamour, I got to enjoy a sweet romance with a girl that no one would dispute had A-list glamour, even though neither of us was anywhere near a red carpet. When Antony, Lee, Simon and I were first signed to the record label, we used to go to a pub in London called the Sugar Reef, where we would hang out and just chat to anyone who crossed our path. The girl on the door was a real gem and long before we had recorded our first record, she made a big deal of us being signed to a label and treated us as though we were already stars. The Sugar Reef was where I met a certain beautiful young lady, one Katherine Jenkins, who soon became my girlfriend. I really liked her and we dated on and off for several months. I used to talk about being a pop star, while she would share her dream of becoming an opera singer. To my untrained ear, she certainly sounded amazing whenever she sang, and it turns out it wasn't just me who thought so. She was fabulous, and we had a great time together, but then Blue took off, as did I, and she went on to find her own big, shining star.

Like everyone else, I was a big fan of the Spice Girls and ever since I'd first seen them, I'd become a little bit obsessed with Geri Halliwell. Back at home in Devon, I'd bought her autobiography, where she wrote that, if she really wanted to achieve something, she would write it down on a piece of paper, which she would tuck into old photo. So I'd faithfully done the same thing with my dreams of getting into the music business. I probably still have some-where the picture of my grandma, with my hopeful letter pinned to the back of the frame. Almost immediately, we were signed by Virgin, which meant that, one, Geri was right – naturally – and, two, I might get to meet her now we were on the same label.

It all happened exactly as I'd wished, and we became fast, firm friends, hanging out together, going for dinner, shopping, gossiping . . . all the usual things good pals do. Geri was everything I'd hoped she would be – funny, no-nonsense, with her head firmly on straight about the whole fame game, and a great help to me as a newbie to the whole celebrity circuit. She didn't just turn it on for the red carpet moments either, although it did seem as though we were always being photographed together. She was there for the very un-flashy moments as well, such as the time I was having a family and friends get-together for my birthday at a Chinese restaurant in Hampstead. We'd hired a karaoke machine and, unfortunately, Geri happened to walk in just as my mother was singing Geri's very own monster hit 'It's Raining Men', which made it look as though we were a family of stalkers, but Geri took it all in her stride, and simply grabbed the mike and joined in. Good times.

When everything started going pear-shaped with the band a couple of years later, she was there for me again, one of the few who could penetrate my wall of weed-fuelled paranoia, assuring me it would all be okay. She also definitely knew more than most about the business of taking your courage in both hands and jumping off that particular cliff, making the jump from band member to solo entity, and her wisdom was invaluable. The press always speculated about our apparent 'romance', but in reality, she was one of the first people I confided in when my life took a more complicated turn and she couldn't have been more supportive.

My first real celebrity girlfriend, though, was Martine McCutcheon, another Virgin Music signing. We clicked immediately. She would phone me up and say, 'What are you doing? Come over and have some pink poo' – what she called her favourite drink, pink champagne. We had a lot of fun together, and there was a moment when we were going to make it official, but I hesitated. I had a secret life by then that she knew nothing about, and I worried about anyone knowing, and about hurting anyone. The kindest thing to do would be to bring it to an end, I decided, before it ramped up into something I couldn't get out of.

I used the time-honoured excuse of us having too much work on, and thinking it would be best to cool it. Of course, Martine's no fool. She just shrugged and said, 'Well, when I'm walking up the aisle, just you remember that if you'd played your cards right, you could have been Mr Martine McCutcheon.' Imagine!

I genuinely really liked all these lovely girls. I've always been attracted to bonkers, beautiful types – strong, assertive women with an unpredictable streak to them. I can relate to women very easily because of my upbringing with my mum and my grandma, and I've always loved female company. I think women are generally kinder than men, or at least, more prepared to demonstrate it, plus, they're more willing to show their vulnerability, which, for an old softie like me, is everything. Plus, more often than not, they're beautiful.

Despite the evolution of my sexuality, or perhaps because of it, I was very drawn to these women – looking back it was perhaps a way of stamping down on my confusion, hitching my wagon to their more confident carts. It can be pretty confusing trying to work out who you're attracted to, especially when lots of dazzling people are suddenly in your orbit, and particularly when you're starting to carry a whole bag of secrets as well. So I was quite happy to be photographed on the red carpet with all these lovely women, such as Martine, Geri and my closest friend of all, Tara Palmer-Tomkinson. I never called anyone my actual girlfriend, but the press were having far too much fun following this 'serial dater' in action to worry about that.

Of course, it helped those reporters as much as it did me. To have me wandering around with that label on my back meant any time I was seen anywhere with a pretty girl within a hundred metres, they could legitimately publish a picture of her as my latest catch, and that sells newspapers. But I admit it also had an effect on me: if you're really struggling to find your own identity, and the press label you very confidently as something, it can be hard to resist playing up to it. It's not really who you are, but it's clearly an aspect of you they've jumped on, so, without having to do very much, you accentuate it and soon become that person. I remember the presenter Fiona Phillips, one morning on breakfast TV, reporting 'asexuals are apparently on the increase'. Earlier that week I'd been on the show with her, and now she ad-libbed that maybe those people just needed an encounter with me, which was 'like having a triple shot of Viagra'. She carried on, 'Duncan reawakened parts in me I thought were dormant.' How could I resist that kind of billing?

Mind you, looking back, I'm convinced many of those seasoned tabloid journalists and entertainment reporters actually had my sexuality sussed, probably long before I was certain of anything myself. Even if they didn't do it consciously, most of them had been in the business a long time, and had seen people like me before. It's interesting that I was never tagged a 'ladykiller' (okay, it's not the sixties), a 'love rat' or even a 'rogue', despite the huge amount of female company I kept – I could safely leave all of that to Lee. Instead, I was given the slightly coy, moustache-twirling epithet of 'ladies' man' – which covers all bases, I guess. I let them get on with it as it didn't seem to be hurting anybody and I thought it helped keep everyone off the scent.

What nobody realised was that in between all those red-carpet pictures of me with my arm around a pretty girl, I was actually protecting a much bigger secret of the heart, one that had caused me as much pain as it had undoubted happiness, and one I'd been carrying around with me for years, ever since the beginning of Blue.

During our very first tour, in November and December 2002, I started getting to know one of the male dancers. He was a beautiful guy called Pete and he became a good friend to me as we travelled around. A very spiritual man, he was always introducing me to new ideas, books, music, everything. He gave me a copy of *The Celestine Prophecy* and I, like millions of others, fell for its profound truths, told in simple stories. Because Pete had given me his copy, I paid special attention to it, particularly the words he'd underlined. I'm not by any means a big reader, so I really should have known then that he was getting more than my usual attention. One day, late on in the tour, he turned to me and said, 'You do realise I'm gay, don't you?' He told me because he didn't want me to freak out about him if I heard this from someone else, but I was actually far too busy freaking out about myself at this point.

Our chemistry continued to develop, and I realised my feelings for him were getting stronger, although I had no idea how to open that particular door, or even if I wanted to. However, by the time the tour was over in 2002 and Pete had moved on to his next dancing project overseas, I realised he'd left a big gap in my life. We stayed in contact by email, me in London, him in New York. Very soon, I decided to visit him there, which is where we shared our feelings for one another. We had a wonderful time, properly fell for each other, and so it began – our secret relationship that would involve meeting in hotels, bars, holiday apartments, lots of romantic hellos and sad goodbyes, all over the world, for the next four years. And not one person knew about it. By then I was one of the UK's most constantly photographed young faces. How we kept our secret, I will never know, but somehow we managed it.

We had our blips. After the first year, I became paranoid about being found out. I used to like being seen as 'Duncan from Blue, ladies' man' and if anyone ever suggested that I might be gay, even for a joke, I panicked terribly, and would get straight on the phone to Pete – 'You haven't told anyone, have you?' The poor bloke never had, but I decided I couldn't live my life this way. I found myself unsure whether I was actually gay, or whether it was just a phase, so I called it off with him. He was devastated, but I became hell-bent on finding a girlfriend, and went into a determined pursuit of a beautiful girl called Anya, who I'd known for a while.

Pete was heartbroken, but I thought I'd made my choice. I fell in love with Anya – she really was a gorgeous girl – and set about getting on with the rest of my life. Well, that lasted about a year before I realised how much I was missing Pete. He'd moved to Los Angeles following our split, and was being very curt in his replies whenever I emailed him, and refusing point-blank to speak to me on the phone. As you may have already guessed, I've never been one to avoid the dramatic option, so at this point I decided to fly to LA to surprise him in person. Because that's always a really good idea, right? I got there, jumped off a 12-hour flight and went straight round to his apartment. At this point, did the violins start playing, the flowers start blooming and everything become once again right with the world? Or, actually, did he sit me down and tell me, 'We can't be in contact anymore'?

I forget the finer details, but I believe it may have been the latter. The reason I have trouble remembering it clearly is because I fell to the floor like I'd been shot and sobbed for England, my heart properly broken for the very first time. At last, I discovered all the emotions, sentiments, fears and longings that Blue, the Brit Award-winning, multi million-selling band I was in, had been going on about in our songs for years, and it wasn't pretty. I was a big, blubbering mess and Pete had to pack me off in a cab back to my hastily booked hotel, before I flew straight home the next day. I'd been crying so much, I wore sunglasses all the way home on the plane, so I looked as much of a dickhead as I felt. What a disaster!

157

The only silver lining to this big romantic cloud was that it finally forced me to address my private feelings. This meant being on my own to lick my wounds, and not involving other people like poor Anya, expecting them to rescue me. I knew breaking it off with her was the right thing to do, but that was awful as well – almost worse, in a way, than my emotional dredging at the hands of Pete. I really loved her, and she was incredibly understanding and sweet, even though I couldn't tell her the real reason for my wanting to part. It was only years later that we spoke again, and I was able to explain properly.

The cycle continued for a while with Pete, however. We'd get back together and have a wonderful time, then I'd freak out, disappear out of his life, be photographed with other people, he'd decide he couldn't deal with that and suggest we split, I'd get upset, plead with him for another chance, until he'd finally agree. It wasn't good for either of us, and I was no happier with myself. Then, one night in LA, it all came to a head when he sat me down again and said, 'Enough is enough.'

Distraught, I curled up in my hotel room and wondered, 'Who can I call? Who can I trust with all of this?' The answer was Simon Webbe, back in London. Simon is the keeper of the secrets. He's always been the most discreet of the four of us, both about his own business and other people's, and I knew I could trust him. Bearing in mind we'd spent such a huge amount of time together over the last five years, living in each other's pockets on tour, getting drunk, kissing girls, swapping stories, this probably wasn't a conversation he was expecting to have. However, all credit to Mr Webbe. If he raised the merest hint of an eyebrow, I wasn't able to tell as I broke down on the phone, sobbing and telling him how miserable and lonely I was feeling. I mentioned Pete and Simon asked very straightforwardly, 'Have you got feelings for him?' I'll always be thankful to him for opening the conversation like that, in such a sweet, non-judgemental way. I told him I did, but it was all over and I was broken by it. And Simon's response? He said, 'I knew something was up with you. I wish you'd talked to me earlier, it hurts me that you've been dealing with this by yourself. I'm here for you, I love you to bits.' He promised me he wouldn't tell anyone, and then he asked, 'Duncan, who's there with you?' As it happened, my mum had come out to LA with me on that trip, and Simon said, 'Go and talk to her.'

At this point, I raided my mini-bar, downed as many single shots as I could find, and went and knocked on my mum's door. She was in bed asleep until I turned up, still crying, saying, 'I have something to tell you.' I sat down on her bed, while she tried to find out what was going on. Finally, I told her, 'I think I might be gay, and Pete's broken my heart.' She burst into tears and replied, 'I thought you were going to say you were really ill.'

She put her arms around me and said, 'Don't worry.' Then she carried on hugging me, told me she loved me and said we'd get through all of this together. She gave me more than I could ever have asked for, although she couldn't help sounding a bit sad when she said, 'Does this mean I'm not going to have any grandchildren?'

Funny she should ask. Three whole weeks later, I was back from that disastrous trip, licking my wounds and on holiday in Cyprus. I'd decided the best way to forget my problems was to go on a sunny mini-break with a bunch of great friends, and I do recommend it for anyone suffering a broken heart. I was in a taxi on the way home from a big night out when my phone rang. It was Claire, telling me, 'Hi, I have something to tell you. I'm three months pregnant with your child.'

Claire? Pregnant? My child? You might well ask. I should probably explain Claire was an old girlfriend of mine, who I'd first met when I was 19 and in my very first boy band, while she was in a Spice Girls tribute group. She'd become my girlfriend then and we'd stayed close friends ever since, with the flame often reignited through the intervening years, including, most recently, during a fun-filled evening at the Lowry Hotel in Manchester, three months before my phone rang in a cab in Cyprus.

She cut to the chase. 'Yes, I'm sure. And yes, I'm keeping the baby.'

So, three weeks after my mum and I had had a little cry together in Los Angeles, I had to go and see her once again. I knocked on her door to say, 'Déjà vu! Guess what, I have something to tell you.' She just opened her eyes wide, clearly wondering what else was coming her way. 'You remember I told you I was gay and you weren't going to have any grandchildren? Well . . .'

Thus, the next, most important chapter of my life unfolded – becoming a father. I came out to Claire straight away – I didn't want there to be any more confusion than necessary in that regard – and she said she'd always guessed, but she didn't doubt my ability to be a good dad. And so we became parents together, when Tianie arrived in February 2005. It's been hard sometimes, making it all work between the three of us, but we've got there somehow. I've been blessed that Claire has always been such a fantastic mother – I couldn't have picked anybody better if I'd planned it. We were like family before, and that's never changed.

I was so frightened all those years about my secrets coming out – it felt sometimes as if I was swimming through an emotional cyclone. And then Tianie came along and it seemed as though she brought the calm after the storm – this beautiful, peaceful baby girl who quietened everything down and made me get a grip on what was, and is, real. She centred me, coming into this world and helping me in so many ways. Becoming a father made me grow up a lot, forced me to stabilise myself. And being a gay man now, I feel incredibly fortunate and grateful that I became a dad by chance like that. God works in mysterious ways.

Over the next few years, I had relationships, good and bad, and had my heart wrenched apart more than once. I became a lot more relaxed about my sexuality, not shouting about it, but no longer keeping it a secret from my closest circles of friends. The lid was rattling on top of the can and it was bound to come off eventually. I was doing musical theatre, for goodness sake!

In 2007, I took part in *Dancing On Ice* and Stephen Gately was one of the other contestants. He'd been a massive boy band star all the way through the 1990s, and then came out as gay in 1999, the year before Boyzone split for the first time. In the changing room one day when we were rehearsing together, he suddenly gave me a big hug and said, 'Duncan, don't let anybody put you down or make you feel ashamed.' It was just what I needed to hear, from someone who'd walked such a similar path – a good Catholic boy forced to face up to the truth and address his sexuality under the beady eye of the unblinking public. Stephen had faced the tougher challenge of coming out a decade before, when people were still far less tolerant, but he had such dignity and carried it all so lightly. I was devastated to learn of his sudden death, two years later, but I've always tried to heed his words.

Then, one day in the summer of 2009, I received a call from my publicist. It was the day I always knew was going to come. The *News of the World* had been approached by someone I'd been with and the bloke was looking to sell his story. I had to decide whether to tell my story myself in my own words, or hope it would go away, but it was out there. I knew this was something I had to deal with, either now or later, and I realised it was probably time to bite the bullet so I decided to do an exclusive with the newspaper and be as honest as possible.

I think it's probably easier now, but it's still a big thing. Back in 2009, it was a lot tougher. The whole week before the story was due to appear, I spent speaking to my family and friends, telling the Blue boys what would be happening, trying to keep myself calm. There were lots of people I wanted to hear it from me first before they saw the headlines. I thought those conversations would be tough, apologising to people for all the lies I'd told, telling them what was to come, asking them not to judge me. I was admitting not just my bisexuality but all the deception that had been part of hiding it. I was frightened nobody would like me anymore, that people would scream at me for lying, or abandon me. But no one did – I received only outpourings of love. I have to say, too, that nobody seemed completely dumbstruck by this news.

Despite all the support I received during that long week ahead of the article appearing in Sunday's paper, I was still terrified about what kind of reaction I'd get – from fans of the band, from new fans I'd made on stage, from other members of the press from rival newspapers. Even without the sexuality aspect, after keeping those secrets locked tight for so many years, I found it completely surreal to be sitting there, describing my innermost thoughts, romantic attachments, fears and desires for the whole country to read about if they so wished. I'm not sure it would be a comfortable sensation for many people but, as I said, the day had come.

One of my closest friends, a lovely man called Boo, could tell I was becoming more and more uncomfortable as Sunday loomed nearer so he came up with a wonderful and generous idea, which was to whisk me away to the South of France on a wine-tasting trip that weekend. We got in the car, crossed the Channel on a ferry and just kept driving. By Sunday, when the paper was dropping on people's doormats all around Britain and lifting the lid on 'the double life of Duncan from Blue', I was a thousand miles away, sniffing the grapes in a French vineyard. My phone was beeping off the hook with texts, but I was too scared to read any of them, fearing outrage and criticism from anyone I hadn't had a chance to talk to. Instead, Boo had to read them for me, and then report their contents. What can I say? My fears were misplaced. There was only kindness, warmth and support in every word from friends, journalists, colleagues in the industry, and many people I hadn't heard from in ages, but who had been moved to send word. It was those messages that meant, when I came back to England a couple of days later, I could hold my head high and respond to the inevitable curiosity that was waiting for me.

One aspect I found interesting about that period in my life was that I described myself as bisexual in that initial interview and often in later public discussions. We've all seen plenty of similar 'bi now, gay later' versions of men publicly coming out, and this can often look like a deliberately designed soft landing. If a public figure describes himself as bisexual rather than gay, especially somebody in a band like me with lots of young female fans, then it doesn't look as though he was completely lying to them all along when he was smiling, flirting, and hamming it up on the red carpet.

Well, I can't speak for anyone else, but I can say, hand on heart, for me, using the word 'bisexual' at the time of coming out was a completely accurate description of how I felt about myself. I'd had beautiful girlfriends in my life, I'd been completely in love with Anya, I'd become a father only a few years earlier and — let none of us forget — I COULD have been Mr Martine McCutcheon. There was undoubtedly a huge place in my heart for women, even if they were increasingly losing the battle for my finer feelings as the years went on.

Perhaps seeing and describing yourself as 'bisexual', rather than a deliberate exercise designed to help other people come to terms with this new side of you, is actually a gay man's subconscious way of preparing himself for what is to come. Again, I can't speak for anyone else, but I can say that, ever since that first day of coming out, there have been no more girlfriends or female lovers for me. It was as though talking about it out loud for the first time helped the sands to shift. Without the worry, fear and secrecy attached to my sexuality, I could explore it for the first time and experience all the happiness, confusion, joy and disaster that comes with life as a gay man, or as anybody else opening up their heart properly.

The decade of living a double life, first as a very familiar face in a massively successful pop band and then as a solo performer, was a time of great confusion, fear, self-loathing and defiance for me, and I'm sure several people close to me suffered some bruises of their own hearts in the process. Young people playing at love can be horribly selfish and accidentally cruel, and I, with my own complications, was no exception.

These are my only regrets about those days, as I struggled to find out who I really was. Looking back now, I realise I had a lot of chips stacked against me before the fame game complicated things even further. My own Catholic guilt, my extremely conventional, almost old-fashioned upbringing, my status as only child leading to all sorts of worry about letting my family down and not continuing the bloodline all made the prospect of coming out extremely intimidating. In many ways, it would have been a lot easier for me to lead a 'conventional' life.

On the other hand, coming out was the best thing that ever happened to me, and I know I'm not alone. I had a lot of positive feedback when I came out, including from people telling me it had helped them to share their own stories. It's so important to take that step to being who you are, even if it feels like a mountain to climb. You have the right to do it, and you should embrace it. It's no one's right to say otherwise. To be who you really are, and not to be frightened or scared is the best gift you can give yourself, trust me.

CHAPTER 13

'I CAN'

Reuniting, Eurovision

2009

ANTONY

I was on a bus, going to play football near Wimbledon, when my phone rang, and it was Lee. 'What are you doing later? Can you meet me in Knightsbridge?' No more detail than that, but I was curious, especially when I heard that Duncan and Simon were on their way too, as we hadn't spoken in a while. When we all turned up at the designated spot, it turned out we'd been invited to appear at the Capital Radio Summertime Ball. Not just any old gig either, but as supporting headliners alongside Katy Perry. Not bad! Kelly Clarkson, Leona Lewis and Akon were all top of the bill, and other names in the line-up included Mark Ronson, The Saturdays and one of my favourites, Lionel Richie. So, all in all, it was pretty hard to resist.

We agreed to do it, and off we went to our rehearsals. It had been a long time since we'd performed as a group, but it really was like pulling on a pair of old slippers when we got together on stage. We were having a lot of fun, and then I picked up a magazine, and it was full of stuff about our forthcoming reunion. Somebody had written, 'Duncan's doing this, Simon's doing that, Lee's up to something . . . and Antony's probably just finished his black taxi round.' Grrrr! Just like that, after all my years of passing auditions, getting theatre roles, working around the country and standing on my own two feet, it was as though I'd regressed five years, and been stabbed in the back again. I was about to head off to perform at the Edinburgh Festival, but that didn't make it into the press. 'Not this again,' I thought.

DUNCAN

Antony will walk into a room, feeling like he's not the popular one. So rather than over-compensate, he'll just shut down and not speak to anyone. He always says, 'They're not here to see me.' Well, they won't be now! I used to get annoyed with him for his negative attitude, and I remember once telling him to snap out of it – 'Stop being the victim. You're not the victim, you can turn it around really easily. People like you.'

ANTONY

They convinced me, and we did the concert, and it was amazing – even if it was held in the Emirates Stadium, and I'm a Spurs fan, but we got over that.

SIMON

We'd rehearsed properly all that week, with dancers, proper styling, and everyone loved it, including us. Underneath the stage, with seconds to go, Duncan even pulled his time-honoured trick – 'I need to go to the toilet.' It was all comfortingly familiar.

We came off stage on a complete high, looked at each other and said, 'Why are we doing solo projects?' We were all contracted at the time to do our own thing, but it was clear where our hearts lay. The members of the press reporting on the event kept asking us when we were reuniting, so they kind of kept the fire burning too.

Antony was the one who said no. He said he didn't need it, and we had to respect that. It was harder for him because of everything he'd gone through before, and he was clearly worried about it happening again.

ANTONY

I just wasn't ready. I was committed to Edinburgh, and it felt like it was time to follow my own star. I knew I wanted to get back with the boys, I just wasn't sure if I was ready for the aggro that came with it. So any idea of a proper reunion was on ice for now, but of course, the bubbles of excitement were beginning to form.

November 2010

ANTONY

I was with my good mate, Tony, driving along Totteridge Lane in North London. Why am I always in some sort of transit when the phone rings and something kicks off? This time it was a phone call from Duncan, telling me, 'Keep it under your hat, but we've been asked to represent the UK at Eurovision.'

What?! Now, I've always been a massive fan of the Eurovision Song Contest, it's been the reason for a massive family gathering in my house for as long as I can remember – Greek Cypriots, what would you expect? But I didn't feel particularly attached to the idea of entering the British part of the competition again, not after my near-miss with Eurovision, back in 2006, when, flying solo, I'd entered what's now called the Song for Europe competition to choose the UK entry. My song, 'It's A Beautiful Thing', had come second. I didn't get to the contest in Athens and I didn't fancy going through all that again. However, it seemed this time was to be slightly different.

DUNCAN

I've always been a massive fan of Eurovision and back in 2009, I even got to announce the results of the UK jury. Even as a child I'd been allowed to watch it – it was the one night of the year I could stay up late – so I had a huge sentimental attachment to it.

Historically, the UK had done well, with winners including Sandie Shaw, Lulu, Brotherhood of Man and those scene-stealing skirt-rippers, Bucks Fizz. But our showing had become increasingly poor over the past decade or more, no winners since Katrina and the Waves in 1997, an embarrassing nul points for Jemini in 2003, and, most recently, poor bugger Josh Dubovie coming bottom with a dismal 12 points. It was time to call in the big guns . . . and we answered.

ANTONY

Dunc reassured me that this time there wasn't to be any public vote, the BBC had already decided they wanted us, the boys in Blue, to restore the nation's fortunes, so we chewed over the pros and cons. I said, 'The cons are that we might come last and we'll probably get slated.' Dunc responded, 'The pros are that we're going to be watched by 100 million people.'

The day before Duncan's phone call I had been given a part in the musical *Footloose*, so I had to take some time to think it through. A big part of my decision was knowing I'd put the kibosh on a band reunion back in 2009, following the Summertime Ball, so I didn't want to let them down again, not for something this big. After two days, I'd made up my mind: I was in.

DUNCAN

Antony was always going to be first in line, whatever his doubts after 2006. I knew there was no way he'd be able to resist the lure of Eurovision once again – he loves it. Simon was initially a bit less sure.

SIMON

Duncan was pulling his usual trick of trying to bend us to his will with his customary whispering enthusiasm: 'Listen, boys . . .'

I said no, but I was out-voted. I know there's four of us, but for some reason it's never worked out as two against two, it's only ever been three against one, which has kept things simple – strange but fortunate, that.

My argument, okay, discussion, with Duncan went something like this . . .

'The UK doesn't ever do well at Eurovision.'
  'We have an established fan base in Europe, so it'll be different this year.'
  'But it's properly Cheeeze, with lots of Z's.'
  'It's going to be seen by 200 million people.'
  'Okay, cool, you convinced me.'

LEE

I remember Dunc called me: 'How would you feel about playing to an audience of 300 million people?' Bring it on, bruv!

DUNCAN

Lee was a bit iffy, until we started writing the song for it together, called 'I Can', and he became really enthused. But I was definitely the one pulling the wagon. I kept saying, 'It's the biggest music show in the world. If we win, we're laughing.' What a chancer!

ANTONY

And so we set off, following in lots of famous footsteps – Lulu and Cliff, Abba and Céline Dion – hoping to do our nation proud, and restore our band's fortunes while we were about it. It was so good being back together – nobody had changed, Duncan was still worrying about everything, but everyone had got a bit wiser, including me, and the laughs were all still there. It just felt right.

LEE

I started taking the whole thing more and more seriously after we began working together in the studio. 'This could actually be really good,' I thought. The song was great, and had all the requirements for a Eurovision banger – short, sweet verses, distinctive voices and a big, thumping chorus. What it didn't have, which divided opinions, was a key change, which loads of 'experts' decreed was sacrilege when it came to entering the Eurovision Song Contest. So many people told me it was absolutely crucial for our success to have one in there, I ended up researching it, and found out that only a couple of the contest's winners in the past decade actually had one – it's just become one of those Eurovision urban myths. I thought our song was strong enough without it and blimey, I was almost out of my range with those top notes as it was! A key change was definitely out of the question if I ever wanted to ride a horse again.

ANTONY

It was so great being back with the boys. The BBC were right behind us – they even made a documentary about our efforts, with words of advice from veterans like Lulu and Cliff, as well as the supreme entertainer himself, Robbie Williams. Even Mr Bee Gee, Robin Gibb, came on it to say he had a really good feeling about us, which was pretty special, considering his track record. Cliff Richard said we should find the song that we wanted to sing, which might sound obvious, but isn't always. The best part for me, though, was being back in the studio with the boys, going back to basics, working with a vocal coach, practising our dance routines. It was like rewinding to the year 2000 when it all began, and it was amazingly good fun, without any of the aggro that had been part of the last months of Blue.

SIMON

That documentary caught on film our first proper live gig in five years. It was the Eurovision qualifier in Malta and we were performing as guests that night. As it turned out, it was just as well it wasn't a competition – we definitely wouldn't have made it to Düsseldorf. What a dog's dinner! We sang one of our old songs, 'If You Come Back', and it should have been pretty straightforward, but that night we realised that, though the bond between us emotionally was as tight as ever, we had some serious work to do as a group of performers. We were still four individuals taking to the stage, not Blue, and that had to change, which fortunately it did.

ANTONY

Oh my life! We forgot the words, we forgot the moves, it was mortifying, but thankfully, it turned out to be the wake-up call we needed ahead of Germany. Fortunately we had a bit of time to get our act together, and jumped straight back into lessons with our tireless vocal coach before we headed off to Europe for a charm offensive ahead of the contest.

DUNCAN

Never mind the vocals, for Eurovision it's all about looking the business, particularly as we were simultaneously planning our comeback. We were all inspired by Gary Barlow's freshly chiselled look when Take That came back after a while out of the spotlight, so we hit the gym hard. It was just as well we did because we decided to go all out and agreed to pose for the front cover of *Attitude Magazine* – the 'Naked Issue', by the way. It was hilarious having the photos taken, trying to protect our modesty in a studio full of people adjusting lights, holding fans, basically behaving like they'd seen it all before, which they most definitely had, and the pictures weren't for the faint-hearted. Simon, being a former model, had a bit of a headstart on the rest of us, but we all put our backs into it, so to speak.

Whether it was the sight of our six-packs or the song itself, all our hard work in the studio and on the sun-bed paid off, and the bookies slashed the odds on our winning until we were in the Top 5 list of favourites. Of course, in an equal and opposite reaction, the inevitable backlash had begun. Phillip Schofield said on live TV that he thought it was a crap song. Even our old manager, Daniel, crawled out of the woodwork to call our decision to compete, 'career suicide, reckless insanity, like Lewis Hamilton entering a go-kart race'. With supporters like that, who needs any competition?

Finally, we took ourselves off to Düsseldorf ahead of the contest. In total, we were there for 10 days, and it was properly surreal. We met these other bands from all over Europe, all these randoms from places like Belarus and Estonia. It was a right laugh. Ireland's official representatives, John and Edward Grimes, possibly better known as Jedward, were there too, bouncing around, and clearly working as hard as we used to, back in the day. Their charm offensive paid off in spades. By the day of the final, they were second favourites to win.

Saying that, we'd not slacked ourselves. We didn't even go out partying in Amsterdam on our European tour – unthinkable, on previous expeditions – and we'd had one little morale boost. On the representatives' bus taking us around Holland, we were the only band not required to carry our country's flag because people already recognised us. I mean that had to mean something, right? Hopes were high.

After days of press, vocal rehearsals, more press, staging rehearsals, it got to the big night. The UK always get a pass into the final, which meant we only had one chance to pull it out of the bag.

ANTONY

What can I tell you about that surreal night? We got to Düsseldorf's Esprit Arena and although we'd spent years on the road playing to audiences around the world, we had NEVER felt an atmosphere like this. Extraordinary costumes, out-of-this-world hairpieces, flags everywhere . . . The pressure was unbelievable, but we had each other to laugh at, and that helped make it bearable. As we took our place on stage between the placards, taking care not to trip over all the pyrotechnic wires, I could hear myself chuckling at how immense this whole thing was. It was basically another fine mess that Duncan had got us all into. At least, for once, he didn't say he wanted to go to the toilet just as we were about to start.

Exactly three minutes later, it was over. The last firework had gone off, our hands were in unison, pointing at the roof of the giant arena, and all I knew was that we'd sung our hearts out in front of 35,000 people in the arena, and millions more tuning in. Then the voting started, and soon it was pretty clear which way the tide was turning, which was most definitely not towards us. I was thinking, 'This is embarrassing, man, we're going to get hammered. We've been pied.' I've always had a nervous laugh – the boys tell me it always happens at precisely the wrong moment – and sure enough on this occasion I started weeping with laughter at the horror of it all. There was no rhyme or reason to the voting. We'd played to German crowds loads of times. *Nul points.* We'd never been to Bulgaria. *Douze points.* What can I tell you? In this game, nobody knows anything. We ended up coming 11th, with a perfectly round 100 points. Better than *nul,* certainly, but still not much cigar.

SIMON

Now I know how Al Gore and Hillary Clinton feel when it comes to US elections. Because, although we came 11th with the jury vote, later, when every single individual vote was counted across Europe, it turned out we'd actually come fifth. Not perfect, but better. The winner that year was Azerbaijan, a song called 'Running Scared' by Ell & Nikki.

LEE

We'd always known it was going to be a struggle getting back together, so we thought we'd be better off embracing Eurovision, with all the framework and exposure it provided, rather than trying to do it completely on our own. This way, we could also say we were repre-senting our country, and hope the UK would get behind us.

Had we known how few – okay, let's make that *none,* of the promises that had been made to us would be kept – I doubt we'd have done it, because we'd gone through all sorts of flack back home, and it didn't look like we'd have anything to show for it.

To be honest, all those people asking, 'What the fuck are you doing Eurovision for?' actually became half the reason we did it. Would you expect anything less? A bit of pure stubbornness kicked in. Perhaps a bit of the Costa gene rubbed off on the rest of us. You don't want to do stuff that's safe, constantly, and if someone says you haven't got it in you to do something, well, isn't that the time to rev up the motor? But we did well, and I stand by it being a good thing for us to do. I'm proud of it, whatever anybody else has to say.

SIMON

The whole thing had been a platform to launch us back into action together, gauge the interest and see if it was worth pursuing. We'd just played to this massive audience and there was far more interest than we'd anticipated, but we didn't have a new album or anything else ready to deliver. But in the months leading up to Eurovision, we got too busy too quickly with the contest itself, so we kind of forgot about looking that far ahead. On reflection, we should have had a stronger plan for afterwards, another single tucked up our sleeves, and perhaps we'd have gone on a different path.

DUNCAN

In the lead-up to the final we'd been the favourites – we appeared on every TV show, the cover of every magazine, pretty much across Europe as well as in the UK. It really was the perfectly staged come-back, if I do say so myself. Oh, except . . . we failed.

Instead, we copped a lot of negative press when we got back and a whole load of 'I told you so'. But despite everything, I really believe we all enjoyed ourselves. Regardless of the outcome, we did it. We sealed our place in the unique cult history of the Eurovision Song Contest and proved that, after all these years, we could still commit ourselves to something 100 per cent once we'd set our minds to it. The bond between the boys was stronger than it had ever been, and it led to a bonkers chapter in our lives as we whizzed around a bunch of foreign cities, doing small but hilarious gigs and lapping up all the fresh attention from people who'd never heard of us a year before. Having been away for so long, we were back in the mix and it was irresistible. We were flying high again and we could always console ourselves that, without even trying, we'd somehow made it big in some of the furthest-flung corners of Eastern Europe. *Douze points* indeed! What can I say? We'll always be grateful, Bulgaria.

CHAPTER 14

'RISK IT ALL'

A Bittersweet Tale of Music and Mayhem

2011

DUNCAN

I met a man coming out of the shower . . . as all good stories should start, in my dreams anyway, but this one's actually true. I was at my gym, where I was introduced to a bloke who was very friendly, seemed to know all about the band, and immediately gave me a big spiel about his management company and all that he could do for Blue. After all those years plugging away on our own, the four of us were ready emotionally to come back together, we just needed the right project. And, just like that, it seemed to turn up, in our laps, all wrapped in shiny paper with a big bow on it, at least if this bloke's 10-carat chat was anything to go by.

He boasted that he had impeccable music connections, particularly in LA, where he promised all sorts of wonderful, big-name things could happen for us. So no wonder I got all excited over dinner, particularly when I was introduced to this guy's day-to-day manager, a bloke full of even more promises. It all sounded too good to be true, so I brought the boys along to meet them both.

ANTONY

Apparently, this second bloke had always been a Blue fan – why wasn't I surprised? I wasn't keen, based on my trusty handshake test. Remember what my dad told me? It's never failed me. If a man takes you by the hand but doesn't shake it properly, and he can't look you in the eye, you can expect trouble. Well, here I had another lettuce in my grip, and I couldn't catch his eye for toffee, but the other boys were far keener. 'What do you think of him?' they asked. 'He's a waste of time,' I answered. To my ears, what was coming out of this bloke's mouth sounded like utter fantasy football: '"I can get you a million-pound publishing deal." Can you really?' But I already knew I was wasting my breath.

I mentioned my concerns to Lee, but he just said, 'Costa, you're always so negative – why are you like that?' He might have had a point.

SIMON

So off we went. We'd already decided to make this album ourselves, go down the independent route, and after all the pitfalls of previous years and the missing millions, we were determined not to make the same mistakes. It makes me laugh now, but we tried really hard. We took ourselves off to business school for six weeks, learning about numbers, so we wouldn't get screwed over. Okay, we were actually sitting in a pub for most of it, with our exercise books open, but we did concentrate.

Our two new 'managers' convinced us we shouldn't cut corners with production. We thought that meant hiring the best we could afford. They seemed to think it meant flying across the world, renting the most luxurious studios imaginable and hiring the most in-demand producers money could buy, or in our case borrow. Because, in order to follow their advice, based on all their experience in the business, we took out a loan to cover all the costs. Not too much, don't worry, just a cool quarter of a million pounds. Just as well we went to business school, I think you'll agree, as otherwise we could have really easily been ripped off. Anyway, almost as soon as the money appeared in our account, it started flowing like water from a dripping tap. I guess everybody who tries to build something from scratch has the same kind of story. You know what it's like when you're refurbishing or something, the experts around you are telling you your house will be worth more later if you just have the foresight to spend a bit more money now and all the while the money's just dripping through the sieve. Well, it was the same with us as we went about booking engineers, producers, everything to do with making an album. We were told the prices of everything, from studio time to engineers, and we didn't really know enough, even now, to question it.

DUNCAN

First of all, the four of us flew to Miami, where we recorded in Drake's studio, no less. Then, Lee and I went on to LA, where we started recording in another top-of-the-range studio, more hi-tech than anything we'd seen before. Just to add to the glamour, we were told Rihanna was working right next door, and we were working with the phenomenal producer RedOne. He looked like he could be a pop star himself, very charismatic, and had already proved himself by channelling Lady Gaga's talents to international stardom. We'd started our career with production powerhouse Stargate, and a decade later it seemed that somehow we'd managed to secure the services of their natural successor when it came to guaranteed pop success.

ANTONY

The music started coming together really quickly, and it was loads of fun being back in the studio with the boys again, particularly with such world-class musicians looking after us. I was amazed at how good they made us all sound, and I thought the material was amazing. However, the Eeyore in me wasn't completely asleep, and things did start to niggle at me – all of us getting up early to turn up at plush studios for a day's work, and no producer in sight because he'd had a late night, that kind of thing – all on our tab, too. Despite how good it all sounded, to me something started to feel not quite right.

SIMON

It was a strange time because the music was coming together so effortlessly – better than it ever had for us. But away from the studio, things were going distinctly pear-shaped. It felt like we were doing our bit, putting in the recording time and making it happen, but everything else was falling apart. Every conversation started with them saying, 'Boys, we need more money for this, oh, and some extra cash for that . . .' Because of how we all are, we were unwilling to confront them and put them on the spot, so things got messy very quickly.

ANTONY

We flew home and finished making the album in London. But what should have been an exciting time turned into, well . . . there are no words. These two music men presented us with a contract, we said we were taking it to our lawyer to have a look, and one of them tried to come into the meeting with us. The only satisfying part of that entire chapter was the look on his face when our lawyer booted him out of the room, citing conflict of interest. Our lawyer, Bob Page, took one look at the piece of paper and told us, 'Whatever else you do, you're not signing this.' Apparently, we would have been handing over our souls on plates for this pair's nibbling pleasure for the foreseeable future, and probably a lot further beyond. Our lawyer called it an 'old-school contract' and said times had long since changed. You've heard about all the lawsuits that went on in the 1990s, when artists tried to get out of contracts that they had signed at the beginning of their careers, how George Michael had ended up in court fighting Sony, and how Prince even changed his name in a bid for freedom? Well, it was all that kind of stuff – sign here and hand your life away. So, of course, we took our lawyer's advice and refused to sign, and that's when it got really nasty.

Because we hadn't signed the contract, instead we were presented with a bill for expenses that looked like something out of *The Arabian Nights*. Legally, we may have been out of the woods, financially, we were in the soup. This expense sheet covered the entire year we'd all been working together – what will become known in the history pages of Blue as the 'Bullshit Era' – during which time we'd apparently chalked up tens of thousands of pounds in expenses, and I knew we couldn't afford to pay it, not on top of the repayments for the loan we'd taken out what seemed like a century before.

I don't believe the day-to-day manager was maliciously out to get us – he was just a dickhead. He probably thought all his big talk would come off if he just said it loudly and often enough. With the first bloke, though, it had definitely become personal. Because we didn't sign his contract, he had an injunction placed on the album, he tried to sue us, and a huge part of our huge loan went in trying to pay him off. Even then, he came after us for future earnings. It just became ridiculous. It would have been funny if we hadn't been so stressed. We put our company into liquidation and thought that might be the end of it – and then he came after each of us individually. The one bit of good news that year was that we had a new manager, Paul Baylay, and he had our backs.

We'd met Paul in Berlin on a night out with Daniel Schmidt, our Universal Germany rep, and he inspired such confidence in us all during that meeting that we realised we really needed him to be our full-time manager. We probably didn't help our cause when we accidentally left him on his own in a bar on that very first evening out together. It was a cracking night but somehow we all wandered off, leaving him at the table – with a £1500 bill to settle. When Dunc phoned to ask him, Paul asked for a weekend to think about it. But Dunc couldn't wait, he just kept ringing him, and Paul eventually said yes, probably just to get a bit of peace.

Poor Paul, he pretty much jumped in at the deep end as far as looking after us was concerned, with all of this going on from day one. It became really difficult trying to pay all our usual bills as well as paying off the expenses, so Paul asked if we could restructure the payments long enough to get the album out and make some of the money back that we'd spent. The guy refused. It felt like bullying on a massive corporate scale, and we were all getting increasingly bogged down in it. A project that had started out with such high hopes for all of us had become a complete waking nightmare. The worst of it was that all the while, this beautiful album, the best, most personal work we'd ever done, was sitting there, unplayed, unheard, unloved. It was like they were showing us the sweetest sweetie jar, but holding it just above our heads – 'Here's what you could have had.'

SIMON

None of us was exactly Gordon Gekko when it came to looking after the pennies. There were stories that we'd spent frivolously in the past, but we really had done our best with the advice we were given when we starting to make the big bucks. It's such a cliché that people forget to pay their taxes, what you don't hear is the conversations that go on behind the scenes. Back in the heady days of Blue, at the height of our success and earning power, we received our first tax bill, and it was for £400,000 each, nearly half a million pounds. Great, no problem – except some wiser soul than us advised us, 'Use your tax money to buy a house, wait for the market to go up, then pay your tax from the profit you make on the house. With property, you'll always make money.' Sounds simple, right? But that was without figuring in the global downturn and the property crash that resulted. Next thing you know, there's negative equity on the house, a big tax bill that you've forgotten all about, and a whopping great load of interest on top. Classic error. We weren't the first and won't be the last people to make this mistake.

The more money you make, the more people offer their unique financial services, the more different ideas you hear . . . You've all seen the envelopes coming through the door offering brand new credit cards or loan agreements. Well, imagine that on a ridiculous scale. How would you work out who to trust, and who's in it to screw you over? Only by trial and error, unfortunately. I'm not a lawyer or an accountant, I barely have a clue about how tax works. I'm sitting there, a big smiling pop star, paying an expert to do all my thinking for me, and he's busy spending my tax money. Or I've spent it. I'd have been far better off going back to my mum's home and asking her to put the whole lot under the mattress – and sitting on it.

ANTONY

Back in the old days, communication between us in the band was sometimes quite weak, as you can tell in how we ended up splitting in 2005 without even properly realising. The same happened when it came to money. Because we didn't sit and compare notes, everyone started getting different ideas about the best thing to do with all that cash.

SIMON

I tried to build a property portfolio, and I also invested a lot in the bands I was supporting. My bills were probably around £20,000 a month at the height of Blue.

ANTONY

My dad said, 'Invest in property.' So I did – that lovely house in Hertfordshire I told you about. Probably not quite what he had in mind . . .

LEE

I bought a music studio, a nice flat overlooking the Thames, a grand piano – oh, and I took my mum to Sandals in the Caribbean. I've always been a bit 'easy come, easy go' when it comes to money.

DUNCAN

For the first years of Blue, we were living a champagne lifestyle on lots of lovely Dom Pérignon money. The problems started after the band split up, when we carried on trying to live like that, but on lemonade instead. But, nearly a decade later, even the lemons had been squeezed dry. So there were old debts, and new debts. And still this bloke was coming after us.

He told our manager, 'I'm going to bankrupt the lot of them,' at which point Paul sat the four of us down and told us privately, 'No, he's not. We're going to get there first.'

Bankruptcy . . . Now that's a loaded word, and I was really worried about the stigma attached to it. It was daggers out for Blue in the press by then. I'm not sure why they came after us, but I guess there must be something in our human natures that makes that happen. When you seem almost untouchable because you're having so many hits and appear so successful, it's hard to get to you, but when you start coming back down to earth, you create holes the arrows can get through. It might even be a British thing, to keep people from getting too far above their station.

Declaring yourself bankrupt clearly isn't an ideal situation for anyone, and we knew the press would have a field day with us, with our previous jet-setting lifestyles, the fact that it was only a few years after our mega-bucks era – we were only in our mid-thirties and still out there performing, so it probably looked pretty strange from the outside. But our advisors sat us all down and explained that, although public perception might be bad, it wasn't the end of the world and at least we could start to get out of this mess. When it all happened, the press described it as us 'walking away from our responsibilities' but it doesn't work like that – you still have to pay all the debt, it's just managed in a different way. You have a bunch of meetings, which feel like your parents going through your pocket money, all very demeaning, but still not as bad as the feeling of the first bloke breathing down our necks. He still got paid, but he wasn't allowed to deal with us directly, so it was worth it for that alone.

SIMON

I filed for bankruptcy after Duncan, and I was equally worried about how bad it would look. People – all of us – are drawn to more negative than positive stories – I think that's just how we're programmed. And it'll always appear next to my name on a Google search. But it doesn't bother me as much as being chased for the money. The first time around, we lost money because we were given bad advice – no biggie. The second time, it was because someone looked us in the eye and said, 'I'm having that.' That hurt. So, like

Dunc, I felt more fairly treated by the receivers than by the guys chasing us. The lawsuits stopped, and the sleepless nights came to an end. Going bankrupt probably saved my sanity.

DUNCAN

Of course, the press had lots of fun with it all – who wouldn't? Especially when they discovered a bank account in the name of Blue had been closed with less than £100 in it. I agree, that sounds hilarious. We hadn't actually been using that account for the most recent tour; it was just sitting there. But the press loved it, more gruesome headlines – what can you do?

ANTONY

For me, after everything I'd been through, I can genuinely say it was all water off a duck's back. Because I'd had my IVA [Individual Voluntary Arrangement] previously with my house repossession, I was able to say to the boys, 'Don't worry, chaps, I'm an old hand at this.' I actually didn't think I could be made bankrupt after all that, because I had no house, no car – I literally only had my trousers to give away. Nonetheless, it happened – more headlines – but still nothing compared to the relief of not having to deal with all the aggro and sleepless nights that had gone before, and having a fresh start. Everyone thinks bankruptcy must be a massive dark sky over your head. In my case, it was the sun breaking through the cloud.

LEE

I had the least amount of personal debt – just one baby piano, that's me – so it took them a bit longer to get to me, but they did it in the end, the swines. My comeuppance came later, after I put my money in one of those fabled tax-avoidance schemes, which I was assured was a great idea. Instead, my tax bill went through the roof and that was it. If I'd known then what I know now, I would have run a mile from it. Hindsight is a beautiful thing.

Of course the government want to discourage this kind of thing from happening, but going bankrupt actually made me better off financially, because the banks were no longer able to chase me for interest payments. At one point, I received a phone call saying, 'We're coming round for your possessions,' and I replied, 'Well, I'm bankrupt and you've had everything, so what were you thinking of taking?' It gets to a point where you literally have nothing to lose.

I do think there's a bigger issue at stake here than just the four of us. We'll always fall on our feet by hook or by crook, but there will be other, far more vulnerable people than us put in the same position, by banks chasing and chasing so people never have a chance to sort themselves out. Of course, the banks get away with it because everyone's looking the other way, or watching *Celebrity Big Brother* or something. But I do feel for people having the squeeze put on them, and the damage it might do to their mental health.

As for me, well, 'tax' and 'bankruptcy' . . . Working in the music industry, those two words seemed like a very familiar pair of old bedfellows. I could console myself that exactly the same thing had been suffered by some of the greats I looked up to. It even happened to my biggest hero of all, Marvin Gaye, so I figured at least I was in good company.

SIMON

The whole experience changed me for the better. Back when I was still a schoolboy, I once tried out for a football team I'd set my heart on. When the letter arrived, I couldn't open it, because it was something I wanted too badly. My mum thinks my fear comes from that day: I got in the squad, but I was never able to open envelopes after that. Years later, at the lowest point of our financial mess, they would sit there, unopened, on the table, piling up, with all sorts of stuff, good and bad, inside. I'd ignore them, just say to myself, 'I don't want to ruin my day today.' But at some point you have to grow up and take responsibility.

So I open envelopes now. Everything's usually fine but even if it isn't, I've learned to deal with stuff before I shake it off. However, even after all these scrapes, I'm happy to carry on being a bit hopeful about things, perhaps a bit naïve. I'm not going to let someone's actions towards me change how I behave. If I'm caught out again, well, that's life.

DUNCAN

I look back and laugh. I got so sucked in, the opportunity just seemed so big – with producers, deal makers, you name it. It was like a lovely big chocolate cake full of lovely layers, which of course meant only one thing, that it was always destined to melt in our hands.

ANTONY

I was right about that handshake. No disrespect to the other boys, but sometimes I think that because they haven't had a constant father figure in their lives, they're a bit more willing to believe what someone says.

I'll never say anything, there's no point. The boys are hardly going to thank me for it. Very occasionally, Webby might say, 'You were right, Costa.' Duncan would never say it.

DUNCAN

We should have listened to Antony. I don't know if it's because of the dad thing or not, but we've always been a lot more willing than him to listen when someone walks through the door. He's sometimes missed out on a lot of good stuff as a result, but on this occasion he was right.

ANTONY

Fair play to Dunc – I'm surprised, shocked even, to hear him say it. But fair play . . .

DUNCAN

Of course, by the time we finally got to release the album, in April 2013, the moment had passed: we were a year too late, Eurovision was over and it was all a bit of an anti-climax. We'd gone into this project deliberately wanting to stay independent, and then ended up fighting tooth and claw just to be able to call it ours. It was a surreal experience, and left a very strange taste in all our mouths. We had this amazing opportunity, and then it just disappeared. It was such a satisfying body of work, and we all ended up going bankrupt because of it. Just bizarre . . .

LEE

It's upsetting to this day that there was so much negative energy around the album, because the actual energy of the music itself is the opposite. We worked the hardest we'd ever worked, we raised our game to match the producers in the room, and you can hear it in everyone's voices.

When Duncan and I were in LA, we wrote together an upbeat track called 'Break My Heart', which we thought sounded more energetic and powerful than anything we'd ever done. The song was inspired by my breakup with Sami, although I have to admit I couldn't be tested on which particular occasion I was referring to. We were on and off more often than a tap. But I remember the days we spent recording it, feeling so confident and inspired. And it wasn't just Dunc and me. All four of us were contributing lyrics and ideas, really personal stuff based on everything we'd all been through separately in the years before we got back together. It felt as though something magical was happening.

SIMON

Plus, finally, we had the maturity of tone that we'd been searching for since the very beginning. We always knew we had it in us, but at the time Blue first formed, it wasn't a sound the record label chiefs were interested in. They wanted a more teen-friendly, higher-voiced, purely pop sound, and so we'd created it on tracks like 'All Rise' and 'Fly By'. Even though we were respected for our vocals back then, we knew our limitations and what was required of a boy band; we were somewhere between the cool of 5ive, and the wholesome charm of Westlife. And yes, we had our share of sitting on stools with microphones and standing up halfway through the song.

In 2011, it was a very different story. We'd had years apart and we brought all that life experience, good and bad, professionally and otherwise, back with us into the studio. That time apart had served us well, and we came back smoother, more ready to learn, to collaborate, more willing to be personal with our lyrics, everything. Ever since the days of 'All Rise' in Norway, I've always loved being in the studio with the boys, making a record, watching songs being created, piece by piece, and this was no different, just better, because we each brought so much. It really was a sweet spot – musically speaking.

DUNCAN

It was an especially emotional time for me. As well as being back in the studio with the boys I loved, I was in love. By the time we were working in LA, I had started my very first proper, serious gay relationship with a man I'd met in America. He was out there with me, which made the whole experience really personal and special. For me, it's all there on the song 'Heart On My Sleeve'.

ANTONY

There was one song called 'Broken' which I had to fight for them to include on the album, and I'm glad I did. For me, we've never sounded better than that – which is ironic, looking back, because that's exactly what we were at that point: broken, and broke.

SIMON

One good thing came out of it all. As I said, we never used to communicate properly with each other, it was always banter and messing around in place of really talking. We kind of took our friendship for granted in a way, in the early days, as is the privilege of youth. But, after all that we went through together, things changed. We became a lot more sincere with each other. It's funny, really. A complete stranger did his best to break us all individually, and he nearly managed it, but he actually succeeded in making the bond between the four of us much tighter. So, in a strange way, I surprise myself by thanking him.

DUNCAN

You know, whatever else happened later, at least one big promise was kept. After all the blarney, we did get to work with Wayne Hector, and the hit-maker didn't let us down. He brought us 'Risk It All', a beautiful song about chasing your dream, your biggest passion, even if it costs you everything. There was something special going on that day in the studio, and I found it really moving, watching the song take shape. Simon stepped up to sing the first verse, and when Lee sang alongside him, I realised why even the critics always used to praise us for our harmonies. I did my bit and then Antony came storming in for the bridge, before the four of us completed the song, all singing together. Our voices had never sounded better, and it made me very proud. The chorus includes the line, 'If you had it all to lose, why would you take time to choose?' How prophetic.

LEE

Why's the album called *Roulette*? Because we always knew we were taking a gamble. In the end, some you win, some you lose.

CHAPTER 15

'BOUNCE'

Back On Our Feet

2013

SIMON

Our return to the stage together coincided with a fresh nostalgic affection for the music of the era when we'd topped the charts, a decade before. I have my theories about all of this, of course. Did I mention I'm a thinker? Well, when I was at school in the early 1990s, people were listening to Take That and loads of other pop bands. But three years into Blue, around the 2004–05 mark, the sounds were beginning to change. People coming out of college were all indie fans – their memories of Oasis and Pulp made them almost hardwired to turn their noses up at what they considered manufactured pop – and it was those enthusiasts who were getting radio jobs, and influencing playlists. Pop music got pushed out. If you weren't an indie band, you were considered no good, and Blue was one of those groups with nowhere to go.

Then Take That made their stunning return and confounded all that kind of thinking with their massive sales, which were pretty much triple anything the indies could deliver. Sure, they had a special ace up their sleeve with the return of Robbie Williams in 2009, but Gary Barlow and co. had already proved themselves a good three years before that. There was clearly a hunger for their kind of music. It was no surprise to me that pop was once again outgunning its rivals for listeners' affections. After all, that's what it's meant to do. That's what makes it pop.

All of this meant that, after Eurovision in 2012, while we were enjoying ourselves back on the road but wondering what to do next, there wasn't a whole load of pop around. One Direction were making great waves with their young, social-media-fuelled fan base around the world, while Adele and Ed Sheeran were charming the critics, but there was no sign of the kinds of groups that had filled the charts throughout the early 2000s. Radio DJs still played all the best songs from that era – by those bands – the likes of Steps, 5ive, Hear'Say and co. – and no wedding was complete without a singalong version of S Club 7's 'Reach'. You know the one. The nostalgia for that time, the enduring affection for those bands, was all there. Plus, of course, people were curious to find out where they were now – how broke were they, what terrible things they'd gone through, how much hair they had . . . All in all, looking back, the whole project seems really obvious and I'm surprised it didn't happen before it did. I'm talking, of course, about *The Big Reunion*.

DUNCAN

We had a new manager by now, Paul Baylay, and a great team behind us with Sarah Chelsom, our PA, and Sandra Mynheer, who runs the Berlin office of our management. As soon as Paul came to us with the idea, it sounded perfect. We didn't know if the series was going to be a hit or not, but we all liked the sound of it – a TV reality show based around six bands who'd all had a lot of success, fame and a string of hits, but had long since disbanded, being brought back together to rehearse and perform a one-off gig at London's Hammersmith Apollo. The other bands included 5ive – well, actually *4our* because their lead singer Jason Brown refused to take part – 911, B★Witched, the Honeyz, Liberty X and our old pals, Atomic Kitten. It pressed all the right buttons for us. I'm very nostalgic myself, and I really like taking part in these kinds of platform shows, where we can be part of something bigger.

ANTONY

What drew me in were the producers' names – Phil Mount and Michael Kelpie, the same guys who'd given us our chance on *SM:TV Live* all those years before. The only thing that gave me cause for concern was when we were told we'd be introduced to the line-up halfway through the series, a few weeks later than the other groups. I asked the producers, 'But we've already re-formed. How can this be our comeback?' They answered, 'Don't worry about that, it'll be fine.' By the time we signed on the dotted line, the other bands were already rehearsing, and had no idea we were coming. 'This is going to upset a lot of people,' I thought.

Sure enough, the first time we turned up at the studio to say hello, there were some blank faces in each of the groups. Edele from B★Witched went on camera to say it wasn't fair on the rest of the bands – she kept saying, 'I don't actually get it' because we'd been performing together again already – and several of them laid into us a bit, probably for the cameras' benefit. I think they thought because of that headstart we'd try to take over. I heard that Tony from Liberty X met the other bands in the pub one night and insisted there was to be no 'bowing down to the altar of Blue-ness' – I'd have loved to be on an altar, but we didn't assume any kind of centre-stage role at all.

Despite these fears, we blended in immediately, and ended up having a right laugh. There was a huge amount of banter between all the bands, especially when we went out on the road following the Hammersmith gig, which formed the series finale. That night there was such a good reception to every single song, and so much warmth and mutual support between the bands, it made every single person involved want to have another bite at the pie. It was a reminder of what the atmosphere had been like back when we started out, with all the bands in it together. You don't really see it anymore, probably because the music industry is full of either world-class acts all flying around in their own helicopters between stadiums, or newbies who've just won a TV talent show and are working all out to get their full five minutes. Back when I were a lad we all got thrown together much more, and it ended up being like holiday camp behind the scenes. We used to throw apples at Westlife when they were trying to do a serious interview, or they'd try to trip us up with a wire if we were filming. The friendly rivalry between all the bands made for some proper quality japes. Like the time A1 pressed every button in our lift on purpose and kept us in it for ages, so we responded by covering their car in shaving foam. It was all playground humour, but it made the day go very quickly. So *The Big Reunion* came at a great time for us, a reminder of an equally precious great time long before, a window onto how good things could possibly be again.

SIMON

There was also quite a lot of squabbling between some of the members of the other bands, and the ones who weren't fighting were shedding buckets of tears about long-ago injustices, ongoing sorrows, all sorts of private pain laid bare. It made me realise that what the Blue boys had – that laid-back rapport with each other we'd always just enjoyed instinctively – was actually quite special, and not something we should take for granted. And singing together again was just brilliant.

LEE

I'm probably more of a purist than the other boys, and I didn't like the contrived aspect of *The Big Reunion* – coming into the show later than everyone else, 'upsetting' the other bands and all that – but I did enjoy it. After the hard work of Eurovision, and the bittersweet experience of *Roulette*, taking part in *The Big Reunion* felt like a walk in the park – having a laugh, banging out the old hits, seeing all the smiles on people's faces.

It was also clear by then we had something very precious between the four of us that we couldn't just throw away as casually, albeit accidentally, as we had the first time.

ANTONY

Somebody equally precious came into my world not long after. Back in 2012, I'd been planning a Friday night in when my old pal Phil had persuaded me to go for one pint with him down our local to watch the first England game in the tournament. Once it had ended, I set my feet in the direction of home, but Phil had other ideas and we somehow found ourselves in the Essex hotspot Funky Mojoe. I felt underdressed – no hairgel – but I thought I'd give it half an hour to keep Phil company. Suddenly I spotted a beautiful girl glancing in my direction. I thought, 'Don't be ridiculous, Costa, she's looking behind you.' I turned round and – birthdays and Christmas! – I was standing in front of a wall. There was no one behind me. So I took my life in my hands, walked over to say hello and the rest, as they say, is history. At least, it's *our* history. From that day on, it's been Rosanna and me, and we became a family in June 2014 with the arrival of our daughter, Savannah.

Her appearance wasn't without its drama. A couple of weeks before she was due, I had been booked to appear as a patient in *Casualty*, which meant filming in Cardiff for a few days. I had it all worked out so I'd be back in Essex in plenty of time to help Rosanna prepare. Of course, the universe always has other plans . . . I was on set, doing my best impersonation of roadkill, when my phone rang. The team were very understanding and 10 minutes later, I was in the car heading back to London.

I dashed into the hospital and headed for reception, about to ask for directions to the maternity wing, when I realised everyone was staring. I'm used to strangers clocking me, usually when I'm caught in the biscuit aisle at Tesco's, but this was a whole new kind of look – more like ill-disguised curiosity and a little bit of shock. Suddenly, I realised – I promise this is a true story – in my haste, I'd forgotten to wipe off any of my *Casualty* make-up, and it's a testament to their award-winning make-up team that even hardened hospital staff were caught staring at my seemingly battle-scarred face. What were the chances?

Fortunately, Savannah's existence has been a lot more peaceful ever since, and now she has a beautiful baby sister in Paloma Valentina. Her arrival in July 2017 was a lot less dramatic – for me anyway, although her mother might disagree. At least I was prepared this time, a lot nearer, and had a clean face, although it was an equally emotional time. These little girls bring only joy to my life. So many ladies around me after all those years with the lads.

CHAPTER 16

'HURT LOVERS'

Reality Bites

January 2014

DUNCAN

Lee had made up his mind and, as you may have worked out by now, once he's made up his mind, that's it. Lee Ryan, the youngest, sweetest but most unpredictable of us all, one of the few people who arrived on this planet without any form of self-censoring filter, had decided it would be a good idea for him to join the line-up for the forthcoming series of *Celebrity Big Brother*. After years of rejecting producers' advances, he finally gave in as a way of making back some of the pile of cash that had been lost in times gone by and, as we could all tell, was clearly very enthused by the idea.

By the time we'd each had a phone conversation with him that hadn't lasted very long but had consisted of about 10 different variations of 'Are you sure about this?' and 'It's going to be fine, bruv', it was clear there was no more dissuading to be done. Lee was all buoyed up by the thought of having a good laugh in the house and making a decent amount of money in the process. I think he'd even promised his mum a new car. So, instead of wasting any more breath, the three of us, with our manager, Paul Baylay, sat down with Lee and tried to give him a few guidelines.

'It's all a big game in there,' we started. 'You can't be an open book because if you are, it's all going to go a little bit wrong for you. Not everyone is equipped to deal with you the way we are, and *vice versa*.'

'I understand all that,' said Lee.

'On the girl front, play it down. You know that whatever you do in there, you'll have problems afterwards,' we said.

'I get it,' said Lee.

'Whatever else you do, don't get into bed with anyone in the house. Just hold your shit together, basically.'

'No problems, boys,' said Lee. 'I've got this.'

A couple of days later, off he went. Or skipped, even. And entered the *Celebrity Big Brother* house handcuffed to a Page 3 glamour girl. 'Christ,' we thought, 'it's started. This is only going to go one way or the other . . .'

LEE

I thought going into the *CBB* house was a great idea – I wanted to show another side of me from the one that had been caricatured in the press for over a decade. Oh, and I also wanted to buy my mum a car. Like everyone else who's ever been in there since the day it started, I thought, 'I'll be able to reinvent myself' – not real-ising, of course, that the producers had already taken care of that. What I also hadn't realised was how much in denial I was about the state of my drinking.

Since I'd broken up with Sami, the mother of my son, the year before, I was constantly worrying if I would be able to see him enough in the future to be a good dad to him, and I was reeling from the rejection, and the breakdown of the family life I'd so recently created for myself.

Following the whole *Roulette* financial debacle, I was sleeping in Duncan's attic in Ealing, so, by the time the offer of *Celebrity Big Brother* arrived, there I was, up in the attic like Quasimodo, still licking my wounds, mourning the sadness of the past, worrying about the future and drowning all my sorrows in a serious amount of alcohol. If I had to quantify it, I could safely say, at that point in my life, I was drinking around a bottle of whisky a night. Yes, I know. Even so, the only time I thought I might have a problem with the stuff was when I walked to the shops one day for a pint of milk. I was about to open the fridge when I felt my eyes wander from the milk to the whisky on another shelf, and five minutes later I walked home without the milk, and lost another evening to the hard stuff. It was all going in the 'wrong direction' as they say, and I'd had warnings from my doctor, but if I'm honest, I wasn't paying them any heed because I wanted to get properly lost.

So, even though I passed the psychologist's evaluation before I went into the *CBB* house, just perhaps, with the benefit of hindsight, I wasn't really in a strong enough mental state to go and live in a claustrophobic environment, with 11 other strangers, for three weeks, with cameras in our faces and situations deliberately designed to wind us up and bring all our inner demons to the surface. I mean, what could go wrong?

From the first moments of entering the house, it all seemed entirely fine. I was handcuffed to Casey Batchelor – a glamour model who seemed a sweet enough girl. We were locked together for two days, so we had to make an effort to get along with each other, or time was going to drag, to say the least. However, that wasn't a problem with Casey. We started having a proper giggle, and she made it clear she had warmed to me. And then Jasmine Waltz appeared and, before I knew it, she was making goggle-eyes at me, too.

DUNCAN

For the first 24 hours, he was very well-behaved, having a good laugh with everyone but clearly remembering everything we'd said. And then it all started to go a bit pear-shaped. And we watched, wondering, 'Lee, what are you doing now?'

LEE

What can I tell you? Having all that attention from two pretty ladies after a lot of rejection and loneliness was like being in a warm bath, and I lapped it up. Throw in the serious amount of drinking that had been going on before I turned up in the house, and my powers of self-control were kaput, and maybe my judgement was a little off to say the least.

I was chatting to everyone in the house, flirting and joking with both girls, basically waiting for the time to pass in as harmless a manner as possible. However, I did suddenly realise what was going on, that these two ladies were deliberately being put in my path, so it looked like I was swapping from one to the other. At one point, I told Casey, 'Leave me alone,' and then Jasmine suddenly appeared from nowhere, wanting to talk to me again. Then, Casey and I were apparently 'evicted', but in fact, the producers put us in a secret room together, which looked like a seedy little hotel suite. She told me she was furious with me, and the next thing I knew, she was following me into the bathroom!

I can honestly say, hand on heart, I watch hardly any television when I'm at home, so I wasn't really tapped into this world. The boys and my manager had warned me there would be a big audience, but that hadn't really sunk in, so I had no idea how many people would be watching all of this, and discussing it. My deepest thoughts the entire time I was in the house amounted to ' Whatever!'

LEE AND FAMILY

'My son Rain came along in 2008, and I fell completely in love with him.'

'My mum had given me the best possible chance at a creative future. One day, she told me to stop doing my homework, saying it was more important I learned the harmonies to 'Endless Love'.'
(Lee with his mum Sheila in 2012)

'My favourite time…' (Lee with son Rain, 2014)

'My whole family knew what I wanted to do, and as far as my dad was concerned, if it meant I wasn't hanging round street corners and starting trouble, he'd support me in all of it.'

'I'd been planning a Friday night in.. (Antony with Rosanna)

'Our daughter Savannah's existence has been a lot more peaceful than her dramatic arrival.'

'So many ladies around me after all th years with the lads.' (Antony with baby daughter Paloma 20

DUNCAN AND FAMILY

'With Tara Palmer-Tomkinson, who I had the privilege of calling one of my very best friends.'

'We've always spoken pretty much every day.' (Duncan with his mum Fiona)

My daughter Tianie brought the calm after the storm, this beautiful, peaceful baby girl who centred me, coming into this world and helping me in so many ways.'

'It's a comfortingly small world. I attended the wedding of my former bandmate Rita Simons when she married Theo Silveston in 2006.'

SIMON AND FAMILY

'When my daughter Alanah properly entered my life, we both love that it came through our dancing, separately but together, to the same tune.'

'My first date with Ayshen was a pub lunch and we ended up talking for 12 hours.'

'Only when you start to really take care of yourself can you truly find it in your heart to lo someone else and have that love returned.'
(Simon with mother Marlene and fiancée Ayshen)

Roulette was a sweet spot – musically speaking.'

'After the budget-blowing decadence of *Roulette,* it was time for a more focused, lean machine to go back on the road.'

'I'm only truly at peace when I'm creating something – whether it's writing, drawing or singing.'

'A surprisingly heart-warming aspect of the whole thing, was how happy everyone seemed to be to see us.'
(Malibu 2013)

'There's nobody I'd rather be here with.' (Kazakhstan 2014)

BIG STAGE, SMALL SCREEN

'*Douze points!* We'll always be grateful, Bulgaria.' (Eurovision Song Contest, Düsseldorf 2011)

'It was a reminder of a precious time lon before, a window onto how good things could possibly be again.'
(*The Big Reunion* Concert, London 2013

'Something my mum passed on to me was being a big softy.'
(Lee in *Celebrity Big Brother* 2014)

'*Strictly* may sound like a strange lifesaver, but so it proved. It brought me everything my body and mind needed.'
(Simon with dance partner Kristina Rihanoff 2015)

COLOURS 2015–2016 AND ON THE ROAD AGAIN

'For all the problems, the disasters and humiliations we've had along the way, every time we get up on stage, they magically disappear.'
(London's Roundhouse, April 2015)

hout all those challenges along the way,
d be half the people we are. What would
we have to say for ourselves?'
(VE Day 70, London 2015)

'I'll always be in Blue, until the day I die. That's where I'm from; it's in my bones.'
(Lithuania 2017)

BLUE

'Just four very ordinary blokes singing our little hearts out.'
(The Colours Tour 2015)

I was young, single, on the rebound and had two pretty young ladies wanting to hang out with me. I wasn't hurting anyone. If I had to articulate my most profound assessment of the situation I found myself in, it would be, 'Oh well, it's a laugh. And it beats sitting on my own in Duncan's attic with a half-empty bottle of whisky and a broken heart.' I'm sure most red-blooded men would have to agree.

DUNCAN

Outside the house, it was clear it was all kicking off. The tabloids were full of it. Lee was on something like 12 front pages during his time in there, including a bunch of other women from his past turning up with their stories to tell. The discussion programmes around the show were all devoted to the so-called 'love triangle' formed by Jasmine, Casey and Lee.

ANTONY

I used to watch the show every night through my fingers, and then phone our manager, Paul, to discuss the fallout. He and our PR lady, Emily Ball, were working night and day to put out the fires, as tabloids and weekly magazines went open season on Lee, with story after story. I made an appearance on *Big Brother On The Side* to defend him and point out what a well-meaning bloke he was outside, but I knew we were losing the PR battle.

DUNCAN

The thing that struck me was how this whole love triangle business completely overshadowed how gentle and supportive Lee was with Ollie Locke during their time together in the house. Ollie was one of the most popular stars of *Made in Chelsea*, where he'd started out having a girlfriend, but was clearly struggling with his sexuality as that show continued. By the time he turned up in the *CBB* house, he appeared very sensitive and quite fragile. He and Lee were having a great chat about it all, and Lee told Ollie really casually that he'd previously experimented with men, and for Ollie not to be afraid or ashamed of anything. Lee's own unique take on it was, 'Everyone's done experimental shit. I'm a well-travelled person!' His kindness in boosting Ollie's confidence was completely obscured by all the other stuff.

Of course, Lee being Lee, he couldn't resist over-egging the pudding. In the middle of his time in the house, he suddenly hinted that even he and I had done something together in the past – wink, wink. Asked if he and I had ever been together, he replied that he slept with me 'all the time'. I remember watching it on TV and thinking, 'Why on earth has he gone and said that? Yes, we've gone to sleep in the same bed frequently in the past, but that's it.' I asked him much later on, 'Why did you say that? It's not true.' His reply was, 'No, I know it's not true. I just thought I'd say something controversial, to hint at something.' Because obviously, during the course of that whole extraordinary era in his life, he really needed those extra headlines!

Sure enough, the next day's front page . . . 'Lee and Duncan have slept together'.

Lee said to me afterwards, all indignantly, 'I never said we slept together, I just hinted at it. And we had that threesome years ago, so technically . . .'

'Yes, but you and I haven't been anywhere near each other.'

'I just thought it'd be funny if I said it, a bit juicier. People always ask.'

'Well, thanks for that.'

'I knew you wouldn't mind, bruv.'

Did I mind? Not really. I just had to explain it to a few curious people, including my own mother, who phoned the next day. So I would like to clarify once and for all, on the life of everyone dear to me and despite what all those headlines claimed at the time, I have never slept with Lee Ryan. Fact. But now I hope you can see what we were dealing with, on national TV . . .

The nightly audience figures were going up and up, both viewers and press were loving every minute, and the series even got extended by an extra five days because it was doing so well for Channel 5. I could see Lee was still having a laugh, when he was chatting with Ollie Locke, or dressing up and having a laugh with Lionel Blair – as you do – but there were signs he was getting upset, when it was all becoming too much for him. Casey's mum [Kim Batchelor] turned up in the house, and told her daughter, 'He's mugging you off,' thanking Jim Davidson for looking after Casey, painting Lee as the villain, which I knew would upset and confuse him. By the time I saw him getting tearful in the Diary Room, I was becoming concerned that he was getting overwhelmed, because I knew he was more sensitive than people realised. It really could have gone either way, and then the backlash came, and we all thought, 'Here we go . . .'

LEE

When I was evicted, I was in a really good mood. The whole show had only been scheduled to run for a total of 22 days originally, so when they announced an extra five, I was filled with a huge amount of anxiety. The walls were starting to close in on me by then. I was finally evicted on the 24th day. It was a surprise eviction so I wasn't really prepared, but I was more than happy to go.

I was surprised, too, to hear all the booing as I came out, but I thought that was a bit of pantomime so I didn't worry about any of it too much. Then I saw my manager, Paul, AND my publicist,

Emily, waiting for me, and they said, 'Lee, we need to brace you.' For what? I phoned Antony, still buzzing from the relief at being out, and he told me, 'You don't understand what's been going on out here.' He tried to explain, but when he realised he wasn't getting through to me, he had to give up, saying, 'Look, go and get some sleep. I'll talk to you tomorrow.'

After the initial euphoria of leaving the house, I was kind of shell-shocked. By the time I got home, I could barely speak. According to what my friends told me later, I sat in the middle of my living room, ignoring all the people who'd turned up to see me, instead just staring at familiar objects around me as though they were from another planet.

The following day, our manager, Paul, sat me down in his office and brought an enormous file of all the news cuttings from the previous three weeks. I was speechless, particularly when I saw the amount of women who had suddenly remembered they knew me, and contributed their unique insight into this important national debate.

It all got very strange. Someone on Twitter wrote, 'If I see you in the street, I'm going to axe you in the head.' The trickle turned into a flood of abuse, and that's when I started drinking again. Paparazzi parked themselves outside my house, the police even got involved because of the level of the threats I was receiving. I couldn't go anywhere, and was locked inside with just Jasmine for company.

In an ill-fated attempt to get some fresh air and give a chance to this reality-TV-fuelled romance, the pair of us took off on holiday to Thailand, where we had some proper fun for the first few days. But the thought of coming home to the same storm of abuse filled me with dread, so we ended up staying out there for nearly three weeks, and that was when the wheels properly came off the bus. It had all been a very intense couple of months for the pair of us, emotions were running high and there was no way this relationship really had a chance of working in these circumstances. Eventually, we had one row too many and I drove her to the airport for her flight back to America, convinced her departure would mean everything would calm down.

So it was a huge shock to my already frazzled system when the attention, so much of it negative, just didn't let up. I'd been through a lot already in my life, particularly the criticism that came after 9/11, and I'm normally thick-skinned and pretty robust. I can generally brush myself off and look ahead of me, but this was too much. The press just went for me. Of this so-called love triangle, Jasmine had disappeared back home to America and so-called normality, Casey was out having a laugh, enjoying her newly boosted public profile, but I was stuck indoors, or getting heaps of abuse whenever I ventured out. What was strange was that during all my years in Blue, it had been girls being nice, blokes being horrible. Now, it was the other way round, with the guys high-fiving me, and girls shouting abuse. I'd been told not to do any interviews to try to explain my side of the story, so I just found the whole thing extremely difficult.

One of those disturbing days I walked with my son into a restaurant, and a woman gave me a filthy look and started letting me have it in the most abusive language you could imagine. I was with my son and I just felt paralysed – if I had to identify one moment that triggered my real downfall, this would be it.

One of my biggest shocks, too, was discovering that people I'd known in the industry for years had joined in turning their backs on me. Six weeks after *CBB* ended, in the middle of March, I was invited to appear on *Celebrity Juice*, which I thought might be a laugh, and a harmless way of reappearing, alongside like-minded people who knew it was all nonsense. So I turned up, and the crowd started booing as soon as I walked out on set. 'Fair enough,' I thought, 'another little bit of panto doesn't hurt.' But then I realised I was getting dirty looks from people on the panel, including some I'd known for a long time. It was like the opposite of those red-carpet events, where other 'up and coming' celebrities turn up and act as though they're your best friend, even if you've never met each other, just because you're all celebrities together. Here, it had flipped over completely, people I'd crossed paths with for years were behaving as though I was a complete stranger. I sat on the panel, isolated, mortified. I was too sad to say anything much, which I'm guessing wasn't quite what the producers had in mind when they booked me. In an attempt to liven me up, before I could say, 'Get me out of here!' someone brought me a whisky, but that didn't do the job. I just counted the minutes until I could get home, and carry on drinking.

Once that lid was back off the bottle, I didn't stop for months. I got into a bad cycle of reading all the abuse on Twitter, responding aggressively to some of it, staying up all night fretting and then curling up in a ball in the morning, hating the thought of getting up. Somebody on social media wrote, 'He's got a great voice, but the IQ of a brick.' I thought, 'Fair enough,' although a brick's IQ remains untested, as far as I know. However, it's probably fair to say I was in a pretty dark spot.

Then, one night, a bunch of us were at a party, we came outside and a female friend volunteered to drive us home. I told her, 'No, you've had more than me, and you're a girl.' I wasn't intending to sound sexist, I was trying to be chivalrous, in my own silly way. That remnant of the old me turned out to be the undoing of the new, even more unstable version – I got pulled over, breathalysed and arrested. Thank goodness no one was hurt, but the destructive behaviour I'd been hell-bent on for over a year had reached its only logical conclusion.

The reports said that I urinated in the police cell. I don't actually remember, but the truth is, I was hoping they would beat me up so I may well have been taunting them to fight me. When people are telling you over and over again you're a piece of shit, you start to believe it. I wanted them to chuck me away and leave me alone. I wanted to get lost. I think you reflect what you're given, so I'd absorbed all the anger and abuse that had been directed at me, and this was how it was coming out. I felt rotten inside. I had this blackness, so much bad energy. Looking back, I was basically bullied by people on the street, the papers, even other celebrities, it seemed. The boys did everything they could to help, but by that time I was unreachable. Simon told me later I looked like a ghost. As he described it, 'You just weren't there . . .'

SIMON

I knew he was suffering, but I wasn't too concerned that he would actually do himself any damage – he loves his kids way too much. But I knew from my own experience, he had to go through it, not round it, and it was a steep, lonely mountain for him to climb.

LEE

I sat down with my solicitor, and he warned me that, with the various charges, I could be looking at an actual prison sentence. That frightened the life out of me. My current lifestyle, tucked up at home, didn't feel particularly free with all the abuse I was getting, but it suddenly felt heaps better than the alternative.

DUNCAN

Antony, Simon and I were asked into the office by our management to discuss what we could best do to minimise the damage. We were like the firemen brought in to extinguish the Lee flames. We spoke to reporters, and went on TV and radio, saying all the time what a lovely bloke we knew him to be. And we were speaking the truth.

LEE

On court day, I got my act together and turned up suited, booted and genuinely remorseful, not just for the way I'd behaved, but for the whole circus my life had become. The boys all turned up as well, giving a smart, united front to the waiting cameras outside Ealing Magistrates Court. Once again, they were all there for me.

Mercifully, the magistrates took a sympathetic view of my sorry state, and elected to fine me and take my car keys away, which seemed more than fair enough. So it wasn't a prison cell for me, but it was time to return to rehab. I'd been there once before, when Duncan had packed me off a couple of years earlier. He'd seen me going through his cupboards one Sunday morning, looking for more alcohol when everyone else was drinking tea and happily nursing hangovers from the night before.

I didn't enjoy my time in rehab that first time. I found it too harsh, deeply intrusive at a particularly sad time in my life when I wasn't prepared to face up to some of the things that came up in the sessions. This was different; this was quiet. The best thing was being allowed to sit in my own room, shutting myself off from the world. I didn't take my phone. I locked my door, and I just had a rest. I wanted to be completely alone, and relish the quiet. I wanted to be lost for a while, but this time without the alcohol, and it possibly saved my life. It put a lot of the nonsense I'd been going through in perspective. I actually enjoyed rehab when I went the second time, and I came out a lot better, but I would never say it's an easy thing to do. It's tough, and you have to wade through a lot of shit that you feel like you could well do without, but you do eventually come out the other side, and then you realise the benefits. There's a Native American proverb I cling to, called 'The Soul Would Have No Rainbow If The Eyes Had No Tears'. I'd gone through so much money already in my life, and now I'd lost a lot of pride, status and dignity along with it. Going through rehab was like having the final layer stripped away. It leaves you bare, but it does give you the opportunity to ask yourself, 'Who am I, and who do I really want to be?' It's like starting all over again.

I've never watched back any of that series of *Celebrity Big Brother*. The thought of it upsets me too much, knowing how it was edited, and the story they clearly managed to tell.

Everyone was treating me as though I was married, either to some poor lady outside the house, or to one of those poor cuck-olded girls inside. I became a 'love rat' but I'm still not sure who I was even meant to be a rat to. I genuinely have no idea why it was such a big deal, particularly in comparison to some of the other stuff that went on in that house, while people were busy getting all hot under the collar over me. That same series, my old *Hell's Kitchen* playmate Jim Davidson was horrible to Linda Nolan, bringing up things from her past with her dead husband in a conversation that left her in bits. Dappy got into a fight with Luisa Zissman; even Lionel Blair was kicking off. It seemed everyone was having their moment, while I was just kissing women and being silly. Looking back, I was just on the wrong show. I should have waited and appeared on *Love Island*, where my antics would have gone unnoticed.

I was definitely a willing party to all that went on, but the two girls were as well. I think Casey genuinely liked me, but I'm not sure Jasmine ever did. These days, Casey and I are cool with each other – we have a good chat whenever we bump into each other. As for Jasmine . . . well, she kept trying to tear more shreds out of me whenever it looked like she might be in danger of disappearing out of the papers. After one of her grenades got lobbed in the press, what did my 'spokesman' have to say that made me giggle? 'Lee wishes her the greatest happiness and success in her aspiring acting career.' Well, I still do.

When I came out of rehab for that second, and hopefully final, time, I was much improved, although I did relapse a bit, a situation not helped when I finally got my own place in Kensington a few months later. I loved the little flat, and it was only when I got the keys and went wandering that I discovered it was above an off-licence and opposite a pub. These things are sent to try us . . . This was a test too far I'd set for myself, and I did slip up from time to time. I managed to stop drinking whisky and moved to wine, until I realised I could easily drink a whole bottle without realising, so I gradually weaned myself off that too. Instead I joined a gym, and eventually started healing myself properly, simply by being alone.

My whole adult life, I'd been immersed in a group, going straight from living with my mum to hitting the road for years of hotel rooms with Blue, and then setting up home with Sami and our son. From there, I'd gone to being curled up in Duncan's attic, before all the chaos and claustrophobia of the *CBB* house. Now, in my Kensington pad, literally the size of a postage stamp, it was the first time I could stretch my arms, touch the walls and know that the space in front of me was all mine. The real solution to all that stress, confusion and finally despair that I'd experienced turned out to be very simple: just some much-needed solitude.

CHAPTER 17:

'WITHOUT YOU'

A Unique Friend in Tara

February 2017

DUNCAN

Behind all the apparent excitement, the exotic locations and glamorous events, I've found one of the hardest aspects of carving out a career in the entertainment industry is finding true friendship. As much as people think you must be shallow because they get this two-dimensional version of you on the stage or on the TV screen, I find it equally challenging trying to work out other people when I meet them. It can become a game of cat and mouse, with both people's authenticity up for question. And then, if you get burnt a few times, as I have, it can be hard not to become cynical and untrusting, which is a shame, because then you risk missing out on the people who are being sincere. For all these reasons, I completely understand why celebrities who are single when they start becoming well known often end up staying that way – where do they start? Equally, I can well see why two people who know each other well would stick together – it must feel so much safer.

One person who cut through all such nonsense was Tara Palmer-Tomkinson, who I had the privilege of calling one of my very best friends. As well as my closest and dearest friend, she was actually my first proper famous one. I saw her properly for the first time on TV, appearing in the very first series of *I'm A Celebrity. . . Get Me Out Of Here!,* and I think I realised then, even through the strange prism of reality TV, what an unusual, thrilling person she was. Bizarrely, through my childhood years – back in Dorset; well-behaved choirboy – I can remember my *Telegraph*-reading grandparents talking about her in disapproving tones: 'That Tara Palmer-Tomkinson, she's a disgrace.' It was strange, my grandparents didn't usually concern themselves with gossip, but Tara – through her royal connections, distinctive name and capacity for making headlines – had somehow broken through the thick wall of their radar and become shorthand for all that was privileged, reckless and naughty about living in West London and mixing in aristocratic circles, at least over the breakfast table in Blandford Forum.

Despite their attitude, or more likely because of it, I ended up paying her lots of attention on screen, and I liked her from the moment she turned up. Then she revealed she'd sneaked some eyeliner into the jungle, and I decided I adored her, this woman after my own heart – suitably bonkers and beautiful. 'I'd love to meet her,' I thought.

Fast forward a matter of weeks, the band was booked to appear on *SM:TV Live* and we were waiting backstage to perform. I spotted a tall lady standing in front of us, about to go on and be interviewed, and to my delight, I realised it was Tara. I went straight up to her and said, 'Hello, I loved you on *I'm A Celeb.*' She was really smiley but seemed quite taken aback, and surprisingly shy. Later, just as we were leaving, she came up to me, said goodbye and shook me by the hand. It was so sweet. In her hand was a bit of paper on it with her telephone number, and that was it. We started texting each other and became fast friends – arranging to go to the same events, dragging each other along to things – 'I'll go if you go'. Photos started appearing of us together, and we began to be invited jointly to stuff, which meant both our individual worlds widened. I brought her on stage at Wembley Arena and she played along. If she was receiving an award, I'd be booked to present it to her. The other boys all got along with her, so she soon became an honorary Blue member. She was my first signed-up, indisputably famous real celebrity friend, and she was almost royal to boot, so it was all quite exciting. She became my 'Shmooey', while I was always her 'Shmoo'.

She could really laugh at herself, too. One time, we all went out to a party at a private members' club after a show. It was meant to be an 'intimate' event, which meant about 20 entertainment journalists duly turned up to report on what we all got up to. The answer was, lots of dancing. Simon was on DJ duties that night, and Tara was one of the very first to head out onto the dance floor. Whatever the press had to say about Tara in the papers, she could charm the honey off them in person. As they watched her trip the light fantastic, she joked, 'Don't worry, I won't give up the day job.' Someone asked her, 'What is the day job exactly, Tara?' to which she replied, quick as a whip, 'I don't know, darling. I ask myself that every morning!'

We skirted on the edges of romance, and she admitted she was a little bit in love with me, but I knew a proper relationship wasn't on the cards because of my sexuality. I was always frightened to have that conversation with her back at the beginning, because I wasn't sure where it would end up, whether our friendship would survive – not because of anything she did, just because of my paranoia about all my friendships at that point. In a different life, if I'd been straight, I think we would have ended up having a very public, intense relationship, although we may have ended up strangling each other too. Instead, we settled into an intimate friendship, where we held each other's hands, and had each other's backs. Our unresolved attraction to each other, plus our shared love of mischief, always gave it an edge, which played out in being really naughty, like two schoolchildren together. Nobody was safe.

Because we were so close, it could make for incidents that were sometimes hilarious and often volatile, occasionally both. One summer, she invited me on holiday to a Greek island, where she had rented a beautiful villa with a pool. When I arrived, the first thing I spotted was the centrepiece in the living room, a beautiful, huge vase, full of giant bamboo shoots – that, and a grand piano over by the window. It turned out that Tara had felt like playing a few tunes, and had had the piano shipped all the way to the villa for the duration of her holiday. As you do . . .

She'd just split up from her fiancé, so she was a bit sad, but desperate for some fun and distraction. The first night, we went for drinks at a hotel bar nearby, where we met some other friends, including Cat Deeley. When we got back to the villa, Tara disappeared for a while, before re-emerging, looking like somebody out of a vintage Hollywood magazine – stunning dress, jewels everywhere, even a hairpiece. Having dazzled us all, she sat down to play the piano, effortlessly bashing out a classical sonata – as was her custom. Suddenly, she realised that Cat had meanwhile gone for a dip in the pool in her underwear. 'Great idea,' shouted Tara, who promptly jumped in too – dress, jewels, hairpiece, everything still attached. After we all started having a swim, Tara disappeared again, to get ready for her third act. Suddenly, the enormous bamboo shoots landed on top of the water. We turned round, and there was Tara, wearing the giant glass vase – completely naked, except for the vase. She literally would do anything to make her friends laugh, and she had proper funny bones.

Of course, this being the pair of us, within days mutual adoration had flipped over into aggro. The press had got wind of our trip, photographers turned up, and we each thought it was the other one's fault. At one point, she got so cross and frustrated, she was lobbing her expensive Boateng shoes at me like missiles, until I spotted a pineapple on the table, and threw that back at her. She closed the door just in time, and the pineapple smashed against it. We carried on screaming at each other, and she threatened to go home. I didn't believe her, and went off to bed. When I went to find her in the morning, she'd gone. Somehow, as only Tara could, she'd managed to conjure up a private jet in the middle of the night, and left the island.

Six weeks later, we still hadn't spoken when we were booked to present a show together. We turned up separately and sat in our dressing rooms in silence. The tension was unbearable and I ended up kicking a door. It came off its hinges, and we both burst out laughing. Of course we made up, as we always did.

Despite her unpredictability, I always felt very safe around her. Once I'd addressed my sexuality, long before I was out publicly, we had no secrets from each other. Over the years, we went through an awful lot together. I was happy to agree no man was worth it any time she was suffering with a broken heart, and she was one of my biggest supporters when I came out in 2009. I couldn't have done it without her guiding voice in my ear, 'You can do it, Shmoo.'

It got harder to stay friends with Tara as the years went by. She wasn't looking after herself, but she didn't want my help, so the times when we weren't speaking grew longer. I'm so relieved that we made up again properly at the beginning of the last year of her life. She had emerged from her dark place, and told me she realised I was a true friend and was grateful for it. I was too. We became as close as we'd ever been, thank God.

Despite her own health problems, Tara proved what an unbelievably good friend she was to me in the summer of 2016, when I ended up in hospital, having back surgery. I'd always suffered from problems with my back. During my first two tours with Blue, I'd had to have epidurals to get through the dance routines in one piece. However, my problems flared up again in 2015 when I got in those heels for *Priscilla, Queen of the Desert*. Honestly, I don't know how ladies, and some blokes, do it! Anyway, I woke up one morning in Bristol and found I couldn't move at all. I knew it was pretty bad and I just wanted to get home. Somehow I got onto the train back to London, lying on the floor the whole time, with people stepping over me in the carriage. I went straight to Charing Cross Hospital, where they gave me an epidural and sent me on my way, so I limped around to see Tara, who lived nearby, and she could immediately see how much pain I was in. I lay down on her living-room floor for hours, and bless that woman, she kept going to the fridge and giving me shots of neat, cold vodka to dull the pain. In fact, I ended up downing so much of it that, despite the agony I was in, I ended up getting the giggles, which set Tara off as well, and soon we had tears of laughter running down our faces. In the middle of a very dark chapter, this was a precious pocket of light relief. She sat by my side for hours, until I could arrange for an emergency MRI scan and got myself to another hospital. There, it all got very frightening again, with the doctors telling me I needed emergency spinal surgery because of a compressed sciatic nerve. They would have to operate within 24 hours, or I would risk having a catheter for the rest of my life, or perhaps not even walk again.

Straight back to Charing Cross Hospital I went, where I had the surgery and thought I was out of the woods – until I got home and started having terrible headaches. It turned out that while they were sewing me back up, they'd nicked my spinal column, and spinal fluid was leaking internally. My body had sprung a leak, and the only way I could survive was by lying down. The doctors weren't prepared to risk operating again, so I had to stay in hospital, lying still, while it hopefully healed. Back home to recover, and another leak from my spine, this time to the outside world. Lovely! Another trip to Charing

Cross, this time in an ambulance with paramedics, who were amazing and did their best to cheer me up, even though I was petrified.

More surgery, more hours and hours of having to lie still while the glue set on my wounds, and Tara remained by my side throughout all of it. It's funny how things work out. Because I was forced to stay in hospital, and because my old friend was prepared to drop everything to come and be with me, those days gave us the chance to connect again properly after all those months of estrangement. Everything was explained, forgiven, and we had conversations of a depth that we hadn't had for years. And we had a laugh too. Tara could never resist causing mischief. This time she hid in the cupboard and gave the nurses a big fright when they came in. Like I said, she had funny bones. Those hours we spent together are really precious to me.

My back still gives me problems, but it continues to heal, while my grief for Tara will never go away. Our fall-outs over the years were enormous, but they came from the roots of an intense, loving, highly dramatic friendship, of the kind that comes along only rarely, and that was at its strongest in the last year of her life. I'll never meet another person like Tara – she was in a class by herself.

I'll always love you, Shmooey.

CHAPTER 18

'BREATHE EASY'

Battles for Health

2014

SIMON

Depression isn't something you can say just started on Thursday, or in May, or even in 2016. It's something that sneaks up on you, like ivy up a wall or something, so that by the time you notice it's got a grip on you, your power to do anything about it has been massively reduced. That ivy's grown over the windowsill, it's in the house.

I was always a deep thinker, ever since I was a child, but I definitely didn't have depression then. I was too busy charging around – mostly doing sports, always hiding from teachers. The same was true of the first years of Blue. I didn't have time to be depressed – too busy catching planes, recording, meeting people, having fun . . . It was only when I sat back, stopped running and actually stood still for a few minutes that it caught up with me.

I took what could be described as a break in any real sense in the four years between 2007 and 2011. I'd saved some money, and I got offers to do different things, but I figured it was time for a rest after the chaos of the past few years. I was thinking about making another album, then not doing it, and constantly giving myself far too much time to think.

I was also indulging, on a massive scale. I partied very, very hard, with lots of alcohol and late nights. Unlike some of the others, I hadn't really gone for it in the Blue years, so I was definitely making up for it now. They tell you, go hard or go home. I went home . . . and brought the party with me. My familiar face could get me into any club in London, and the invitations were overwhelming. Or, if I didn't feel like venturing out, my flat had an open-door policy. From Thursday night to Tuesday, I became the host with the most. I maybe took Wednesdays off. I was sleeping all day, partying all night, keeping the hours of a vampire. And I found absolutely no purpose in any of it – I was a deep thinker living a shallow life. This went on for about two years. For six months of that, I barely left my bedroom. The party around me continued, I just didn't see it. There were people wandering around my flat, so I'd just open the doors and leave them to it.

What was I missing? Someone to keep an eye on me, instil confidence in me, tell me everything was going to be all right. But that person didn't exist, or I hadn't found them. Through my years recording solo stuff, I'd got used to providing the paycheque, the instructions, the reassurance, whatever was required . . . Everyone looked to me for guidance, but I never actually wanted to be top dog, instead I was faking it as an alpha male.

I should have been seeing my family more often, because that would have been grounding. But when I did go and see them, I'd cry all the way home, thinking, 'Why don't I see them more often? I can't wait to see them again . . .' and then I'd leave it for another six months.

I didn't tell anyone about it, because I saw my anxiety as a sign of weakness. And I remained in a state of denial for a long time, thinking it was a phase; that the old me would just appear again one day when I woke up. I only acknowledged I had a real problem when I started riding motorbikes, and wondering what it would be like to speed up and take an impossible corner. I was playing a form of Russian roulette with myself – if you survive, you'll do well; if you don't, then you don't want to be here, anyway. I forced myself to think of my daughter, my mum, my brother, everyone I was close to, and how bad it would be for them if I harmed myself. And that stopped me doing any real damage, but it was a close thing.

The boys saved me. During our long history together, everyone in the band had always come to me, but I'd never really gone to them. I'd mention the odd thing, but the boys knew me well enough to leave me to sort out my own problems. But now, they feared something bad was going to happen to me, and they didn't want it on their consciences.

DUNCAN

Simon is a very private person, and he keeps it all in. Lee, Antony and I all wear our hearts on our sleeves, but he's a lot more guarded. But we felt that he was going on a downward spiral, abusing himself, and we all started noticing. We didn't say anything, and he wouldn't talk to us about it, until we finally felt forced to step in.

SIMON

The first time they brought my problems out into the open was on a trip to Miami in July 2011, when they all sat down one evening to talk to me. They all said, 'You have to slow down, you're hurting yourself. You need help.' Duncan was the most direct. He told me, 'You've lost your colour, you look grey.' I just broke down.

DUNCAN

He broke down in front of us for the first time ever, which was very strange for all of us. Although he was in a lot of pain, it was actually quite lovely to see him like that in a way, because it made him more human and real to us. And then when he began opening up to us, for once we were able to help him, in return for all the hundreds of time he'd always been there for us over the years.

SIMON

Things didn't improve straight away, though. In fact, one night in Kazakhstan, I'd nominate as the darkest before the dawn. We'd been booked to perform in the country's capital, Astana, after an invitation at the personal request of the President. All went well until everyone else went off to bed, but I still wanted to party. Apparently, I was being really aggressive, walking around without my shirt on, asking people for fights. The boys told me the next morning that security had called our manager Paul at 6am, after they found me lying on the floor of the hotel bar, still ready to fight the world. Apparently they walked me to bed. The most frightening thing of all was, I couldn't remember one moment of it – I'd had so much to drink, I'd had a blackout.

What I do remember, horrifyingly, is trying to open the windows in my hotel room, high up on the 10th floor. I was intent on getting out, but for the first time in a decade of touring, the windows were locked. When I got back to the UK, the memory of that played over and over in my mind, and really scared me. Soon after that, Lee phoned to check how I was, and I admitted, 'I'm lost, man. I don't know where I'm going.' And he said, 'Just hang in there, stay focused, get yourself back together, because something good's going to happen. I can feel it.' I held onto his words for dear life that day. And they came true, because the very next phone call I received was an invitation to appear on Series 12 of *Strictly Come Dancing* in 2014.

From the bunker of despair I'd been in, that may sound like a strange lifesaver, but so it proved. It brought me everything my body and mind needed – a clear framework, a reason to get out of bed, get to the gym and let the endorphins do their magic. More importantly than anything else, it gave me a goal. Slowly, a glint of sunshine appeared where it had been very dark for so long. I took it day by day, doing exercise, eating properly, looking after my body, and gradually my mind stopped whirring.

Strictly gave me something physical and challenging, and I really hoped I'd be good. Kristina Rihanoff was the perfect partner, and I didn't want to let her down, either – I wanted approval from her and from everyone watching us.

The car appeared to be back on the road, and I kept myself together until the fourth week onscreen, when – to my horror – I found myself crying live on national television. I'd bonded during our weeks of training with my fellow contestant, rugby player Thom Evans, and suddenly we were up against each other in the bottom two of that week's show. Somebody would be going home, and I was overwhelmed by the prospect that it might be me. When Kristina and I discovered we were going through to the following week, that's when the tears started, and they didn't stop. I let it all out. It was a surprise as much to me as to everyone watching. I thought, 'Well, the cat's out of the bag now,' and that's when I decided to talk about my depression to the press. The support was immense and life-changing, more than I could ever have hoped for.

One thing I've discovered through all this is that only when you start to really take care of yourself can you truly find it in your heart to love someone else and have that love returned.

I first met Ayshen Kemal at a celebrity football match years ago. I was there because of Blue, and she was in a band at the time called

Fe-nix. I spotted her straight away and she stood out for me because, unlike a lot of people at these kinds of events, she didn't seem in the least bit interested in mixing with other celebs, she just wanted to kick the ball around. 'That's my kind of girl,' I thought. I naturally made enquiries, but it transpired she was with someone, so I left her in peace.

Our paths crossed a lot in the years since then – going to the same gym, bumping into each other on the train, having a little chat, keeping my feelings for her well hidden, all the usual stuff. Then, two years ago, we were both single at the same time, so I asked her out on a proper date. I was feeling more confident about myself by then, so hearing 'No' from a girl was just about okay, but fortunately that didn't happen. Our first date was a pub lunch and we ended up talking for 12 hours. The second date, I invited her to come to Hong Kong with me. She was a bit freaked out, but I told her, if we didn't get on, we could just watch the films on the plane. Fortunately, that didn't happen either. It turned out she had always thought I was 'that idiot from Blue' but eventually I was able to talk her round.

Life is full of surprises. I never thought I'd have enough to offer anybody to go down on one knee, but that's what happened in February 2017, on the last night of our holiday to Jamaica. I would have done it earlier, I'd been hiding the ring for four months, but people had been talking up our prospects, and I'd wanted to catch her on the hop – judging by the pictures we took, I managed it. For once, Ayshen was speechless. Usually, she's got her head firmly screwed on, and she keeps mine screwed on too. I'm in the happiest place of my life right now.

So I feel recharged, but I'm not healed. Depression doesn't just go away. It's something I'm aware of every day, a big monster knocking at the window, sometimes tip-tapping, sometimes banging, and it can still hit me when I least expect it. Ayshen seems to know instinctively when it hits me, and she just quietly lets me know she's there, while giving me the space I need to get my head into a better place. Everybody is so different, I would never dream of telling anybody else what to do, but for me, I've realised my happiness is dependent on making a series of small decisions every day, turning on that mental ignition as soon as I wake up, and sorting out my mind so that everything's in the right place. And then it's off to the gym for me. Exercise and plenty of water are my fuel.

People in my position do need to talk about this. It's a duty. No more people should be lost to the kind of despair that I felt. The pain comes from keeping it inside, and I did that for too long.

All I can tell anyone going through anything similar is that I'm not a natural speaker, as the boys would tell you, but the times I didn't share, it got worse, and when I did, a huge weight came off my shoulders. The actual strength doesn't come from the reaction you get, it comes from the decision to open up. The strength you need is already inside you – you just have to let it out.

I FF

Unlike what Si describes, my problems with my throat were completely self-inflicted, let's get that straight. Anything I suffered I can directly trace back to the alcohol I'd been drinking so much of for so many years. I have only myself to blame, and doctors to thank.

We were due to go on tour in 2015, and as we were preparing with rehearsals, I suddenly realised I couldn't sing a note. I could still speak, but when I went to form a musical note, nothing came out. Pardon the pun, but I was almost speechless with shock. Through all those years of hard partying, screaming in nightclubs, shouting at Duncan, I'd never lost my voice. My voice has become lower than it was when I was a teenager, but it's still there. Or so I thought.

I took myself off to the doctor, who did some tests and told me I had a cyst on my vocal cords. Apparently, this can happen if you simply over-use your voice – I know, I *know*, even this little mouse! But lifestyle – all right, smoking and drinking, let's be frank – can definitely play a part. Of course, I immediately jumped on the internet and according to what I read, I was expecting to be given medicine to dissolve it. I thought I'd be back in action within weeks. Not so fast, grasshopper.

The doctors told me that the affected area was larger than normal, so the usual treatment wasn't going to work, and instead I'd need steroids. They put me on a course to last three or four months, and – there's no subtle way to describe this – I blew up. So now I had two problems to deal with, I'd lost my voice and possibly my live-lihood, and I was a Weeble.

People started telling me to my face, 'You've put on weight.' I thought, 'I've actually got more problems than that,' but I didn't let on. I was drinking a special honey and lemon tea with more nutri-ents in there than you can shake a stick at, but the steroids failed to do the job. I wasn't happy when the doctors told me that, as a result, they'd have to perform surgery to get rid of the little devil. I imme-diately imagined every worst-case scenario that went with having a pair of scissors near your vocal cords, but there was no alternative. So I had the operation and all went well, until they took away my little throat visitor for diagnosis and called me in again for 'a little chat'.

My doctor sat me down and told me, 'Everything's fine, but it almost wasn't. If you'd left this any later, it would have become cancerous. The cells were changing. We caught you.' Hearing this made the blood drain from my face. It was a proper, ground-coming-up-to-meet-me kind of shock, which I'm sure was the doc's intention, as he said it deliberately harshly. I'd still been drinking and puffing up to that point, taking it as seriously as I take everything, i.e. not at all, but that conversation was what kicked my arse into shape. I'm still no angel, but I definitely started looking after myself.

Even after the operation, I had to stay on the steroids while my vocal cords healed, which meant I continued to look like a tyre. Strangers would make comments when I least expected them. At one point, I was up to 15 stone, and I was at an airport with the boys. I was trying to hide it with big clothes, but a woman came up to me, specifically going out of her way, just to say, 'You're a lot fatter in real life, aren't you?' The real surprise was that, out of everyone around me that day, it was Simon — quiet, relaxed, respectful Mr Webbe — who lost it in response. He turned round and snapped at her, 'He's been on steroids for cancer in his throat.' I thought, 'Blimey, Si, calm down.' It was a bit of an exaggeration but it did the job. She made some sort of bumbling apology and wandered off.

You never know what you're going to say to someone that might affect them for the rest of their life. People do think they can say whatever they want to famous faces, though, and I don't think they're even trying to be rude, it's almost a nervous reaction around someone you've seen off the telly. I'm sure that same woman wouldn't go up to a complete stranger and start having that conversation, but she thought she could with me. Oh well, what can I say or do about it? I've had worse.

Having those problems with my throat made me reconsider my relationship with singing, though. I'd been belting out big tunes since I was eight years old, and hitting all those high notes was something I just took for granted, until my voice could no longer deliver. On the one hand, being a singer had saved my health — it was how I'd noticed the problem in the first place — and on the other, I'd caused all sorts of problems for myself and singing was the one thing in my life, beyond my children, that had brought me more happiness than anything else. I'm only truly at peace when I'm creating something — whether it's writing, drawing or singing. It was time for some payback. So I took myself off to school. For the next year, I worked with an amazing music teacher, who gave me the technical tools to support all the things I'd always done instinctively, and gave me a fresh appreciation for the privilege of being able to express yourself through music. Since applying myself like that, I've felt more content than in many, many years. What am I without my voice? It's what keeps me happy when I'm sad. It's an integral part of who I am, it just took nearly losing it for me to realise.

CHAPTER 19

'NO GOODBYES'

Older, Perhaps Wiser

2013 and Onwards

ANTONY

By 2013, with the help of our manager, Paul, we'd finally pulled our heads out of the sand, started to recover from the whole untidy mess that was bankruptcy, and begun operating as a much more efficient business. After the blindfolded budget-blowing decadence of *Roulette*, and the financial disasters that came with it, it was time for a more focused, lean machine of a band to go back on the road. We sat down and agreed, 'Let's do what we're good at, which is getting out there and giving people a good evening out.' We just had to cross our fingers that there were enough people out there who still wanted to hear us and see us in action.

DUNCAN

And, bizarrely, despite all the put-downs and jibes in the press – particularly when we handed them that gift-wrapped-with-a-bow present of all of us going bankrupt – it turned out there were. We'd already decided that we weren't going to be precious about the kind of gig we did, or even whether we got a rapturous reception, we just wanted to do a good job, have a laugh together and get on with it. It's amazing how financial disaster can focus the mind like that. So that's what we did, but the added bonus, and a surprisingly heart-warming aspect of the whole thing, was just how happy everyone in the crowd seemed to be to see us. In 2013, we ended up performing at 176 shows all over the world.

ANTONY

I have to say, since we got back together properly, there have been some strange invitations. I don't know if Paul hides the more bizarre offers, or if they're the ones we end up accepting, but it's made for some pretty random excursions.

DUNCAN

Back in the days when we first had success, all the different countries we visited passed by in a bit of a blur – if it's Tuesday, it's Hungary, that sort of thing – and we didn't really ever get to meet any of the locals properly apart from in the most controlled environments. These days, travelling as a much smaller unit has made for some pretty unusual up-close-and-personal encounters, far less controlled, and we've learned not to look surprised whenever we go somewhere new.

SIMON

If we've had some heart-warming moments, there's been the odd heart-stopping one along the way, too. One time, we were invited to perform at a gig in Ulan Bator, which I had to look up on a map. It turns out to be the capital of Mongolia. You knew that, right? We were standing in for the Backstreet Boys, who'd had to cancel, and it was a bit of a hike to get there, all told. We flew to the Canary Islands for one TV show, then to Barcelona for another, then to China, and finally on to Mongolia. It was at Beijing Airport that things began to get a bit hairy. A huge fog had come down, and Duncan got out a pack of cards in the departure lounge. He started playing Patience, saying out loud, 'If this comes out, we'll make it there safely.' We all asked him a few times, 'Could you not do that?'

ANTONY

We got into a bus to take us onto the tarmac and drove past lots of lovely shiny, big, new planes. Each time I thought, 'This must be us,' but instead we kept driving. The driver didn't stop until we'd reached the very edge of the airfield and we were faced with an ancient, tiny old Boeing, like something out of a black-and-white war film – paint stripping off, one wing Sellotaped back on, the works. And when we climbed on, well . . . Now, I'm normally a big fan of an ashtray, but even I thought, 'How old IS this thing?' We were all pretty quiet as we took off, passing through the thick fog until we reached clear sky, where we could easily see the moon and the stars. Beautiful!

I looked at the boys – Duncan and Simon plugged in with head-phones, eyes closed, Lee typing away frenetically on his laptop, putting another idea for a script on the page. Everyone happy. Then I glanced out of the window and saw what I thought were some stunning fireworks going off over the city. I pointed them out to Paul and he went strangely quiet, particularly when the plane turned in that direction. I looked out again, and d'oh, we were flying straight into a lightning storm, which was why the tiny plane started bouncing like a ball. Next thing I knew, the captain's voice came over the speakers, asking everyone on the plane – that would be all five of us then – to buckle up. He actually said it twice, but we didn't need telling the second time. Even the ladies who'd been calmly pouring the coffee put their cups away and sat down with frowns on their faces.

It was properly terrifying. I was sweating buckets, Duncan had reached for his cards again, and even Simon opened his eyes, which was when I thought we might really be in trouble. Only Lee seemed immune to the whole thing, knees up on the seat, no seat belt in sight, still tapping away on the keys. 'What are you writing about?' I asked him. 'A plane crash,' he replied. 'Let me read it to you . . .' 'Er, maybe another time, bruv.' But it worked. Lee had turned the switch on my nervous laugh, and I started chuckling. Then somebody else, I think it was Simon, muttered, 'Flipping Backstreet Boys . . .', which set us all off. We caught the air hostesses staring at us, which just made us giggle more. Bear in mind this was when the plane was being buffeted around the most, pulling up and then deep dipping, like a tiny boat in a rough sea. What a sight we must have looked, all gripping each other by the hands, one minute screaming, the next laughing, until the tears ran down our faces. By the time we'd flown through the worst of it – a very, very long 15 minutes later – we'd all wept buckets of laughter at our ridiculous predicament, much to the poor stewards' complete confusion.

DUNCAN

What made it even more surreal was the reception we received when we finally landed in that tiny thing. We staggered off the plane, exhausted but slightly euphoric to have finally made it back to earth in one piece, to discover that we were as big in Mongolia as we were in Bulgaria. Okay, nearly. Fifty photographers surrounded us at the airport, we were herded into blacked-out people carriers, and given – I kid you not – a police escort to our hotel. Our hosts even slaughtered a goat for our arrival, so we could have a big ceremonial spit roast.

ANTONY

It got weirder. Twenty-five thousand people came to the show, and the screams were as loud as anything we'd ever heard back in England. Who knew we were so big in Ulan Bator? Hilarious. Even funnier, it seems there aren't many Health and Safety laws to contend with over there. At our soundcheck, we'd noticed a bloke rigging up some fireworks around the stage. Our manager made them promise not to set them off until after we'd come off stage. Cut to the gig, and we were about 30 seconds in when . . . you guessed it. Bang! Off went the fireworks almost at our feet and out went the lights in the entire stadium. We stumbled our way back to the dressing room and waited to go back on, but it was all over. The gig had to be postponed until the next day due to technical failure, and it sounded like the whole city was booing out there. Twenty-four hours later, back on stage, no fireworks, and screams even louder than the night before. Bonkers.

Before we knew it, it was time to go home. After the caper getting there and nearly being set on fire by some enthusiastic Mongolians, we decided to push the boat out and opt for a shorter journey back, and a much bigger plane.

LEE

Of course, when we got back to London, we knew better than to try our luck and ask for limos, or even cabs, to get us back home. Antony and I left the airport together, and he caught a coach back to his home in Essex, and I got on the Tube. Never let it be said that we still have any ideas above our station. I remember sitting on the District Line, looking at everyone else going about their business, wondering how they'd all spent their weekends – 'Get up to anything much?'

ANTONY

Crucially, I remember sitting on that plane as it bumped around, looking at the others and realising, there's nobody I'd rather be here with. And that's true to this day. We've been through so much together that, whatever happens now, good or bad, aeroplane journeys included, it's just one more thing.

If we were all the same sort of people, it'd be boring. In another life, we'd be four guys in the pub together on a Saturday night. Often the reason that kind of social group lasts so long, from your teenage years and on through the decades, is that no one moves away and nobody gets a better offer. But we've all been all over the place and had plenty of offers, and we still like each other the best.

DUNCAN

Looking back to when we first got together, we just got lucky with who we met, that there wasn't one rotten apple in the cart. But the nurturing of it, that's the result of us making decisions that prioritise each other over and over again, and working at it along the way.

Now, there's so much love and respect, it's almost a weakness, because if there is an issue, we won't talk about it, or if we do, we all want to back down, as we're all equally conflict-averse. Usually, in a group this size, there's one dominant male, but the moment any one of the four of us starts to get het up, the rest of us all back down. We seem to know instinctively when it's our turn, and when it's not. It's like some subconscious mechanism of power sharing, so there's never any head-butting or fighting.

SIMON

We have had a row – one time, in 2003. Four blokes were due on stage at Birmingham Arena, two were on time, and two were late. Can you guess? In fairness to Lee and Dunc, they were on their way, but they got caught in terrible traffic coming from Manchester. They had to go back and get on a helicopter to get to the concert, while Ant and I were standing in the arena, being booed by the crowd because we were so late coming on. This was backstage. We didn't get as far as the stage. By the time the other pair got there, Antony and I were so wound up, we didn't talk to them during the entire show.

Some bands don't talk to each other for years. Our sulk lasted a whole three hours. It was horrible, the worst feeling, and it affected all four of us. Afterwards, we all cried, hugged each other and agreed, 'Let's never do this to each other again.' What a bunch of softies, or new men, depending on which way you look at it.

But it's not like we've had to try hard to avoid confrontation. Nothing grates. If one of us gets on someone else's nerves, it becomes playful. If someone says something obnoxious, someone else says, 'Whatever' and we all move on. There's no malice. We genuinely enjoy each other's company. Other people have always told us how unusual that is for a group that have lived in each other's pockets and still spend so much time together, but for us it's normal. I'm not a family-orientated person. I did a lot of growing up by myself, which has made me a loner by nature. But if I want to go out for dinner, it's the boys I still phone. If I go to the West End, it's to see one of them. My mates are the people I call up, those ones I don't see all the time, but can pick up from where we left off, even if that was a year ago. Those are my friends, and the boys are family. I've met other wiser, smarter people, but they didn't fight for me to get into this band, stay by my side when the chips were really low, when the press tried to pit us against each other and when I was suffering in silence, and can still make me cry laughing now.

DUNCAN

Over the years my respect for Simon has only increased. He's an amazing man. I will always know that he has my back, he's like the brother I never had. Even though there's actually only a week between us, he's a much older, wiser soul.

Lee will always be my bonkers younger brother. He's had his share of scrapes, but he's got himself together, and is a lot more centred than he's ever been. He's still a whirlwind, but it's channelled now.

There's nobody better than Antony – I just wish he'd start to believe that himself. I tell him I want to install a chip inside him to give him the confidence he needs, because he's so talented. When he's feeling down, he behaves like an outsider – he hangs back, and doesn't interact. When Ant's happy, he's in a different league from the rest of us – quicker, funnier, more imaginative. It's quite something to behold, knowing both those sides of the coin are part of the same person.

LEE

I've always loved Antony, and he used to be one of the most frustrating people I know. His issues with self-esteem used to hold him back, and then he let the chip on his shoulder get the better of him and he'd kick off. I guess that's his Greek fire coming out of him.

SIMON

Antony's more rounded these days. When people thought he had a chip on his shoulder, it's because they didn't listen to what he had to say. But all these years later, he's learned to speak up.

ANTONY

The balance between us is so much more equal now. I've learned to be more assertive and say my bit. Before, instead of saying anything, I'd sit simmering silently, so when I did speak up, it seemed like I had a bad attitude. I'm definitely more black and white than the others in my opinions, and I'm very direct. I didn't need to change what I thought about things, but I definitely needed to change the way I expressed those thoughts. So I did, and the others started to listen.

People don't give Lee enough credit. He's a talented boy, and he's written some fantastic songs, but let's just say his decision-making has sometimes led him astray. Occasionally, he'll admit something's his own fault. When Lee wants to talk deep, he'll call me, and we'll sit down for hours. We go back the longest, and I'll always be there for him.

SIMON

Lee's still bonkers, but there's more of a light about him now. He's coming into his own. Perhaps we all are.

ANTONY

Si has always been the supportive one. We've been roommates, and we have a special bond. He knows what I'm thinking before I've even opened my mouth.

LEE

Simon and Antony are both very laid-back and chilled out. Duncan and I have had a few run-ins – never properly fallen out, just bashed heads. We can get on each other's nerves, but it's because we're so similar, both a bit childlike. I remember a journalist years ago describing the four of us as 'famously fatuous, but equally lots of fun'. Once I'd looked up what 'fatuous' meant – 'silly, foolish, childish . . .' need I go on? – I'd say this was still a pretty accurate description of one half of the group. To this day, we're both still hoping to get away with stuff, both hoping Simon and Antony will roll in and tidy up the mess. They always try.

SIMON

Duncan realises these days he doesn't have to be a lone wolf. He's always been anxious about knowing where he stands with certain people, but with us he knows.

ANTONY

Duncan's changed a lot. He used to be the one people went to because of the charm, the good looks, the people-pleasing patter . . . He was always the first port of call. But he had to learn lessons from idiots who've waffled their way in, trodden on him and then gone. I used to think, 'Dunc, don't put yourself out there to be shot down.' Meanwhile, the three lads he grew up with are still by his side.

DUNCAN

When we first split up, I felt safer being by myself. But now, I feel safer with the boys. What they give me is security. When Tara died in February 2017, I was away in Lithuania with the boys the following weekend, and they looked out for me like family. That's what we are, a family. I'm an only child, and Antony, Lee and Simon are the brothers I've never had.

I'm sure there's a price to pay for such a tight bond. Being in Blue, you each take on a bit of Lee, a bit of Si, a bit of Ant, a bit of me.

We are quite vulnerable people   big hearts, soft shells. We react to stuff, and sometimes we over-react. We're reliant on each other, so it only takes one person to go wrong, and it all falls down. But that's the risk that comes with putting your life in other people's hands.

SIMON

It probably stunts our maturity as human beings, but we know that. Everybody wants to stay a kid forever. Especially boys. And what better way to do it than by staying in a band that you formed when you were little? Turning your boy band into a man band.

But we do need each other. We're happier together, and it actually makes us more creative, even though it feels less like work and more like fun. So I figure we might as well build our professional model around what makes us all feel the most content.

ANTONY

Even now, I fear I'm going to be ignored when I'm on duty as part of Blue. I'm not at my happiest in that environment and there are things I think I'd rather be doing, but the love and friendship I feel for the boys overrides that discontent. Being with them, doing a gig, messing about, is still the best feeling, and I forget my worries then. That's the glue, that we still have a laugh, and it remains pure and surprisingly untarnished. We have 17 years of history, and nothing in that time clouds our friendship, so there are no bruises, no scars; no elephants in the room. What's weird is that before we split the first time, when we were a famous group, our names always associated with each other's, I didn't feel part of a team, but now, even though we spend far less time together, I actually do. The bonds were formed young, but there's a truth and honesty with each other that wasn't there before.

The paradox is that by moving further apart from each other, we've become far tighter-knit than ever. Before, it might have been a team on paper, but it had chinks in it. By moving further apart and being able to appreciate what we have, it's become real.

SIMON

Our friendship is something we've been graced with, but we've had other, harsher lessons to learn along the way. To be in a band where every single person goes bankrupt after selling millions of records is a pretty unusual distinction, possibly unique, but it's made us all a bit more responsible, hopefully, about what and who we invest in.

DUNCAN

I wish I'd been wiser from the start about that. I did my best, I just didn't know enough. I've never been good with money, but experiences . . . I wouldn't change a thing, I've loved it all. Oh, apart from wearing those high heels for *Priscilla*. But that's it.

ANTONY

I'd have just spoken up earlier, and I'd have trusted my gut. I'm a lot more careful about who comes into my life now, I try not to let my ego be flattered, and I have an agent who believes in me to the point where he'll tell me the truth, even if it's not something I want to hear, because he has my back.

LEE

It was a reality check coming back together, because success had been relatively effortless the first time around. Back then, we'd worked our arses off, but we had loads to show for it The second time saw us working equally hard, clawing ourselves back up, and then having us all go bank-rupt. What was valuable about that experience, and Simon's always telling us to remember the positives, is that it made us question whether we were doing the right thing by working together, and the answer was, and always is: 'Yes'. Plus, losing all that money has made me realise that if I ever get it back, I'll try to hold onto it a little more carefully.

Everything else I've gone through, self-inflicted or otherwise, I like looking back on it, from the perspective of this final chapter, for now anyway. The good, the bad, it's all made me a better person. If I didn't have those colours in my life, well, it just wouldn't be very colourful, would it?

ANTONY

Without all those challenges along the way, we wouldn't have a story, this book would have blank pages, and we'd be half the people we are. What would we have to say for ourselves? Same band, same songs, different hairdresser. Instead, it's been . . . interesting.

DUNCAN

We can't escape our past, but it's also a legacy. For every disaster there's been a massive triumph – a platinum-selling album, a record-breaking gig somewhere. The challenge now is to remember we have nothing to prove. We did it all as a boy band when it was there to be done. There's no way to match that kind of success as an older group, and we could break our backs trying. Instead, we have to work out how best to enjoy what we're doing, keep it fresh and somehow bring our music to those people who want to hear it, just like every other person working in the entertainment industry today, really, except with a bit more baggage.

Everyone in the group has their own solo stuff going on now, but I'm all for another trip on the road, perhaps next year. It's such good fun, and I have a fresh appreciation for it these days. I used to get sick of singing all the old songs but after everything we've been through, I just feel grateful to be doing it now, and to still have some people happy at the end of it. I don't need screams anymore, just claps will keep me happy.

LEE

For me, the enduring popularity of those songs brings its own pressure. I've always loved delivering those high notes, but my voice isn't what it was, due to my surgery and years of hurting it before that, and I feel like I struggle on some of the high-end songs. I'm the kind of person who, if I can't do it right, I won't do it at all. I never want to become the kind of entertainer who points the microphone over to the audience for all the uphill lifting. The boys and our manager are always telling me that's rubbish, my voice is better than ever, that I just have to believe it.

The thing is, it's not all about me, anyway. Our music still seems to bring a lot of people a lot of joy, including my bandmates. Who am I to get in the way of that?

Because I'm always looking forward, sometimes I forget how much we've already done. I did have to laugh when I joined the cast of *EastEnders* in early 2017. I thought I was only going to a meeting, it turned out to be an audition, and they cast me as bar manager Harry 'Woody' Woodward the next day. Anyway, the producers pulled me in for the standard chat they give everyone. They sat me down and said very seriously, 'Be prepared for a new level of celebrity.' Haha, like Tony Blair, they clearly don't read *The Sun*.

ANTONY

I definitely feel I have the most to prove even now, and I'm still earning my stripes in the theatre world, so in that sense it's like being back in Blue again. I look on every role as being the audition for the next. When you're in a band, there's nothing beyond it. This gives me a purpose.

The four of us remain more supportive of each other than people ever believe. If one of the lads wants to go and do something on his own, we all say, 'Good luck to you, smash it.' We always did. What's changed is that I won't sit here watching *Jeremy Kyle* anymore, waiting for them to come back. I used to turn other stuff down, but no longer. However, what gives me the confidence to go out there on my own is the lifelong friendship between the four of us, it's one of the great foundations of my life.

LEE

Whatever happens, I'll always be in Blue, until the day I die. That's where I'm from; it's in my bones. Whatever I might want to do by myself, I'll always get on stage with the boys. It's the price you pay for being part of a family Sometimes you have to do things that you might not feel like, left to your own devices. But I know it's also my security blanket against the world.

SIMON

I see something else coming out of Blue, but perhaps that's just hope speaking. I think we're best off playing the long game. Ebb and flow. Go away, do our own thing, come back. Whatever happens, I know we'll always have each other's backs. Plus, whatever each of us put into our individual projects, we all know there's nothing like sharing a stage together, or even just hanging out. It's home.

DUNCAN

Whatever else we get up to, I think we all know it's where we belong.

SIMON

I always knew there'd be longevity with Blue, but also turmoil, both of which have come true. When we started out, I just wanted to get off the streets, grab this opportunity with both hands, make sure everyone around me understood the chance we'd been given and keep everyone grounded. The other three saved me by bringing me in, and I wanted to save them from the industry, and sometimes themselves.

We all know how lucky we were to land in that situation when we were starting out. Anything else that has ever come our way since then really is gravy. We were told back then, 'You have to understand what you're signing up for.' But I already knew, and I was willing. Any ideas I had, about the right to privacy, freedom, as it turned out even my dignity later down the line, I knew all of that was out of the window. It's the price you pay for the chance to do something you love every single day. Faced with that, what would YOU do? I'm signing. It's why, even now, if someone stops me in the street, I always try to have a chat. If I can't because I'm in a rush or something, I feel bad, because these people who want to talk to me are the same people who've given me such a wonderful life. Sure, some less wonderful stuff – more, shall we just say, interesting stuff – has also happened along the way, but if you can learn to forgive all that, and look for the good instead of the faults in people, life becomes a lot easier. I'm not perfect, but I'm not going to let anyone drag me down.

DUNCAN

We've been put down so much by music writers, journalists, former fans, even people on social media, that sometimes it makes you think, 'Maybe we really were that shit.' Maybe it's been our mistakes along the way – not putting our money under the mattress during the first chapter of Blue, not releasing an album after Eurovision during the second, not locking Lee in a cupboard so he couldn't go onto *CBB* – that define us, rather than our music, the laughs we had and the fun we brought to people. Because we're all Brits from the place where everyone loves a 'has-been', you have to work really hard to stop and remind yourself of all the records, the awards, the gigs around the world, the number ones, the fans in so many places.

But more recently, I've realised it's the knocks as much as the triumphs that have kept us closer to people's hearts than we would otherwise have been. While only the four of us really know what it's like being in this particular band of Blue, who hasn't had money problems, sadness, romantic disasters, moments when they've put their foot in it? We just got to live it all out in front of you. So while there'll always be haters, there's some respect, too, just for the fact that we're still standing, still singing, still a bit stupid . . . most importantly, still together.

Because we've all done so many things, our faces are all pretty familiar, and we often get nods of recognition in the street, but I can tell people aren't really sure sometimes who they're nodding at. That all changes when it's the four of us together– people stare and smile. It's like performing a Jedi mind trick. It's been years since we last troubled the charts, but somehow the Blue bubble continues to work its magic on unsuspecting bystanders, even with people who've clearly never listened to any of our records – they're either too young, too old, or far too cool – and I can tell you that the same force field has never failed to boost the individuals within it. We've done gigs when one person's been missing and there's only three of us up there, and it's fun but it's not the same. It only really works its proper spell when it's all four of us together. We are definitely more than the sum of our parts.

LEE

My mum always told me this was going to happen. She read the cards, and they told her I was going to be in a boy band with three other blokes and we were going to be famous, both for good and bad reasons. I spent years wondering what those three faces would look like, and then they appeared one day, and that was that. I think it's why my solo singing career failed, because I subconsciously sabo-taged the whole thing. I wasn't meant to turn my back on my brothers, and I wasn't meant to be on my own. It wasn't written that way. I loved the boys too much – still do.

DUNCAN

Lee's had his share of trials, but we all have. By the time we got back together, all those tornadoes going off in our heads had calmed, and we've never really looked back. And, despite all the mayhem, the madness, the money problems that have come with it, I think we're all incredibly grateful for it – even Antony, who pretends to hate it.

ANTONY

I didn't used to appreciate any of it, but I do now. I never take what we have for granted. For all the problems, the massive anxieties, the disasters and humiliations we've had along the way, every time we get up on stage, they magically disappear and, for one song or 10 songs, it's just four very ordinary blokes singing our little hearts out, having a laugh and hoping the crowd are enjoying the show. And every time we come off stage, we hear the shouts, the claps, still the odd polite scream, we wipe our faces, look at each other and you can tell we're all thinking exactly the same thing:

'We really could keep doing this forever, or at least another week. After all, anybody got any better ideas?'

We rest our case.

'Curtain Falls'

Thank You . . .

What began for us in 2000 and continues today has become a story that you are able to read in this book. Our story would not be complete without all the people that along the way have contributed in parts great and small. People that helped shape us, guide us, inspire us, support us and sometimes just laugh with us through the ups and downs we have lived and breathed. It is impossible to name everyone, so if by chance we have omitted anyone that had a role alongside us then we are truly sorry but rest assured all support we have received over the years means a lot to us.

The roles of everyone involved have been important and we start by thanking Hugh Goldsmith for his vision and belief, and Daniel Glatman for his guidance and leadership (more on that below). To Ray Ruffin, you were a musical inspiration, an incredible talent and we miss you greatly, you left this life too soon. Tor Hermansen, Mikkel Eriksen and Hallgeir Rustan; you created Stargate and you shaped who we were musically and for that we are forever grateful. To Mich Hansen (Cutfather), Wayne Hector, Steve Duberry, Brian Rawling, Gary Barlow, Lee Brennan, Elliot Kennedy, Angie Stone, Ali Tennant, Conner Reeves, RedOne, Lucas Secon, Jonas Jeberg, Ali Zuckowski, Martin Fliegenschmidt, Jez Ashurst, David Jost, Kiko

Masbaum, Robin Grubert, Paul Barry, Taan Newjam, TroyBoi, Tracy Young and everyone that has worked across our five studio albums, three greatest hits, one live album and one EP to date we salute and thank you. To Sara Freeman; you travelled a long way with us and we will never forget you. To everyone at Virgin Records across *All Rise*, *One Love* and *Guilty*, you watched us grow up and we hope you enjoyed it as much as we did, with special thanks to Alison Parry. Thank you Ashley Tabor at Global & Capital FM for the comeback stage you gave us. To Daniel Schmidt, Tom Bohne, Sandra Seefeld, Marietta Harder, Dirk Schömbs, Nora Otto and everyone at Universal Music Berlin, thank you for your belief and hard work on *Roulette*, and to our partners David Gresham Records in South Africa, JVC in Japan, and not forgetting the incredible Henry Semmence and his team at Absolute Marketing in London. To Nikki Downham and Phil Savill for their work at Sony Music, and everyone at INgrooves Germany & UK. Thank you to Simon Jones, Melissa Nathan and Emily Ball, who no doubt lost a lot of sleep but worked tirelessly to keep us both in and out of the press in good times and bad from *All Rise* to *Colours*.

To Gareth Brown, Chris Webb and Nick Tyson and all the musicians, tour staff and crew that have joined us on stage and off across more than thirty countries, behind every spot light (Dave Cohen) and mixing desk (Jimmy, that means you!). To Jeremy Hewitt at Global Merchandise, thank you, and Paul Roberts for all your work on our early tours. To Marvin Smith and Ryan Saklofsky, thank you for your spectacular work on the Colours Tour, we are truly grateful, and to Elizabeth Honan and Terry Bull on the Roulette Tour(s). To Sol Parker who was there from day one creating the biggest shows and even bigger tours, Mike Malak (Coda Agency), Paul Franklin (CAA), Billy Wood (formerly of WME), and Thomas Matiszik (Contra), thank you for the tours, festivals, shows and good times. To Will Blake and Levi Jackson (formerly of Live Nation) thanks for the madness, dedication and utter belief to help us put the machine back on the road again in 2012.

To all the artists we have worked with – Elton John, Stevie Wonder, Angie Stone, Kool & The Gang, Lil Kim, Tom Jones and Lionel Richie – you made our journey unique and complete.

A very special thank you has to go to Johnny B, the man who walked the world with us as Tour Manager and was the last man to go to bed and the first to wake up no matter what corner of the world or Wembley Arena we found ourselves in. Johnny, you kept the path ahead of us clear and shared a lot of the fun along the way. Thank you. In our very first year, two guys from Northern Ireland, gave us our first shot on television in the UK on SM:TV and how could we know that twelve years later our paths would cross again on The Big ReUnion and Blue Go Mad In Ibiza. To Michael Kelpie and Phil Mount, you guys are legends and we will always be grateful for the television opportunities you provided. You will always be part of the Blue family.

To Sarah Chelsom (The Chinch), a woman who loves holidays and festivals in equal measure, thank you for always being there for us with that Chelsom smile. To Sandra Mynheer at 25M in Berlin (our second home) *vielen dank für alles*, see you in the raucher lounge, we love you! To Max Dodson, who has managed to be alongside us since day one, thank you for the iconic photographs, album covers and the memories. To Sandra Ludewig and Phil Griffin for your photographic work and videos. To Caroline Watson, and not forgetting Lydia, Gemma Shepherd and Mads Ronnborg, people who have dressed and styled us more than most; thank you. Thanks also to Bob Cunningham, Stephanie Taranu, Maarit Nimela, Marcos Gurgle, Ayishat, Guy who drove us many miles, Joe Bennett and Steve Tandy for your radio expertise. To Bob Page at MGPH, Paul Spraggon at SSB, Leo Dawson at Lee&Thompson, David Sleight and Maya Silva at KingsleyNapley for providing the right legal and contractual framework when needed. To Michelle Roycroft, thank you for your professionalism and all your hard work. To Stevie Lange, Daniel Thomas and Yvie Burnett for keeping our voices in shape. To James Penfold and William Van Rest at ITV, thank you. To everyone behind the scenes – and there have been many – who kept us moving forward; James Gallimore, Amanda Barnett, Zoe Lengthorn and Lewis Pullan your work and dedication has been appreciated. To Alastair Thomann (you're crazy but we love you), André Guettouche, Sönke Ingwersen, Kristina Kuntz, Daniela Forster and Max Abele, thank you for the fun and great memories from Frankfurt to Hong Kong and back again. To everyone at Bell-Lomax, especially Lauren Gardner and our new family at HQ/HarperCollins including Rachel Kenny, Lucy Richardson, Alison Lindsay, Louise McGrory and Celia Lomas. And of course none of this would have been possible without Caroline Frost, thank you Caroline for your vision, your voice and unwavering determination.

Several people have claimed to have managed Blue but there have only ever been two managers that have guided us: Daniel Glatman and Paul DH Baylay. We had a small bump in the road between Daniel and Paul that we have covered in detail in the book and needs no mention here. Daniel's vision, hard work and broad shoulders means we would never have been who we are without him. Thank you Daniel, who could have imagined back then just really what was being created. Thank you also to Paul, you stepped in when we were neck deep and you balanced the ship again, not to mention took us places we couldn't even point to on a map (the 25,000 people who came to the show in Mongolia will never be forgotten). And who could forget the magic of Taormina, Sicily on the Roulette Tour? Your belief in us is incredible, your positivity an inspiration.

Of course none of this would have been possible without our families, partners and now our children, who, as they grow older, never cease to inspire the belief we carry.

Finally, Blue would never have been Blue without the fans. Many of you have been with us since day one, others have joined along the way but wherever and however you found us, your support made us who we are. We hope you have enjoyed the journey with us and our love for you will never diminish. Thank you for the shows, the albums, the tours and everything in between.

In addition . . .
Antony would also like to thank his parents Mike and Andrea, brother Louis and sister Natalie and everyone in the family for their untiring support through good times and bad, and Rosanna, Savannah and Paloma for their love. To David and Sue, thanks for everything! And to Bill Kenwright for the belief.

Duncan would like to thank his mother Fiona, Claire Grainger and his daughter Tianie for their love and support.

Lee would like to thank his mother Sheila for the encouragement to follow his dreams.

Simon would like to thank his mother Marlene, his fiancé Ayshen, his daughter Alanah. And Darren, Monique and Quinton. Family is everything.

Photography credits

Plate 1: 'The Early Years'
Top left: Antony – copyright © Andrea Costa
Top right: Simon – copyright © Marlene Webbe
Bottom left: Lee – copyright © Sheila Ryan
Bottom right: Duncan – copyright © Fiona Inglis

Plate 2: 'The Early Years' (continued)
Top left: Simon, Marlene and Janet Dinwiddy – copyright © Karl
   Smith
Top right: Antony – copyright © Andrea Costa
Bottom: Duncan – copyright © Fiona Inglis

Plate 3: '*All Rise* 2000–2001'
Top: Blue in August 2000 – copyright © Getty Images/Gareth
   Davies
Bottom: Blue in 2001 – copyright © Getty Images/Fred Duval
   2000

Plate 4: '*All Rise* 2002–2003'

Top: Blue at the Brits in 2002 – copyright © Getty Images/Dave
   Hogan 2002

Bottom: Blue with Elton John in Germany 2003 – copyright ©
   Getty Images/Franziska Krug

Plate 5: 'Brit Awards 2003'

Left: Simon at The Brits in 2003 – copyright © Getty Images/
   Dave Hogan 2003

Right: Blue at the Brits in 2003 – copyright © Getty Images/
   Dave Hogan 2003

Bottom: Blue at the Brits in 2003, holding award – copyright ©
   Getty Images/Dave Benett 003

Plate 6: 'The Best Of . . . 2004–2005

Left: Blue in 2004 at the Scala Electric Cinema – copyright ©
   Getty Images 2004

Right: Blue backstage at Party in the Park, Hyde Park, London,
   2004 – copyright © Getty Images/Dave Hogan

Bottom: Blue at Pop City Live in 2004 at Ocean, Hackney –
   copyright © Getty Images/Jo Hale 2004

Plate 7: Blue & Friends

Left: Duncan with Geri Halliwell – copyright © Getty Images
   2004

Right: Paris Hilton, Simon Webbe and Diana Jenkins – copyright
   © Getty Images/J. Vespa 2005

   Bottom: Blue with Ant & Dec – copyright © Getty Images/
   Dave Hogan 2001

Plate 8: 'The West End Years: 2006–2010'

Left: Duncan performing with Sheridan Smith in *Legally Blonde*, London – copyright © Getty Images/Robbie Jack (Corbis) 2010

Right: Antony performing in *Blood Brothers* – copyright © Getty Images/Chris Jackson 2006

Bottom: Simon performing with Whoopi Goldberg in *Sister Act*, London – copyright © Getty Images/Neil Mockford

Plate 9: Lee & Family

Left: Lee and Rain in 2010 – copyright © Getty Images/Tony Woolliscroft 2010

Right: Sheila Ryan with Lee at the Tesco Mum of the Year Awards 2012 – copyright © Getty Images/Ferdaus Shamim 2012

Bottom: Lee and Rain in 2014 – copyright © Paul D. H. Baylay 2014

Plate 10: Antony & Family

Top left: Antony and family (parents, brother Louis and sister Natalie) – copyright © Antony Costa

Top right: Antony and Rosanna – copyright © Getty Images/Mark Robert Milan

Bottom left: Antony on beach with partner Rosanna and daughter Savannah – copyright © Antony Costa

Bottom right: Antony with daughter Paloma in 2017 – copyright © Fay Andrea

Plate 11: Duncan & Family

Top left: Duncan and Tara Palmer-Tompkinson – © Getty Images

Top right: Duncan with his mother Fiona Inglis – © Fiona Inglis

Bottom left: Duncan with daughter Tianie – © Duncan James

Bottom right: Duncan with Rita Simons and Theo Silveston at their wedding in 2006 – © Jaine Airey

Plate 12: Simon & Family

Top left: Simon with daughter Alanah – copyright © Getty Images

Top right: Simon with fiancé Ayshen – copyright © Getty Images/Tom Purslow 2016

Bottom: Simon with mother Marlene and fiancé Ayshen – copyright © Andrew Timms

Plate 13: '2012–2014'

Top left: 'Hurt Lovers' video shoot, Germany – copyright © Paul D. H. Baylay

Top right: Simon and Antony – copyright © Paul D. H. Baylay

Middle left: Lee and Antony, backstage at the SSE Hydro Arena in Glasgow – copyright © Paul D. H. Baylay

Middle right: Blue filming a segment for Germany's Next Top Model in Malibu, USA in 2013 – copyright © Paul D. H. Baylay

Bottom: Blue at press conference in Astana, Kazakhstan – copyright © Paul D. H. Baylay

Plate 14: 'Big Stage, Small Screen'

Top left: On stage at Eurovision Song Contest, Dusseldorf 2011 – copyright © Getty Images/Sean Gallup 2011

Top right: On stage at *The Big Reunion* concert 2013 – copyright © Getty Images/Brian Rasic 2013

Bottom left: Lee at *Celebrity Big Brother* 2014 final – copyright ©
Getty Images/Karwai Tang 2014

Bottom right: Simon performing in *Strictly Come Dancing* 2015 –
copyright © Getty Images/Tony Woolliscroft 2015

Plate 15: 'Colours 2015–2016 and On the Road Again'

Top: Blue performing at London's The Round House in 2015 –
copyright © Paul D. H. Baylay

Bottom left: Blue on VE Day 70, London in 2015 – copyright ©
Paul D. H. Baylay

Bottom right: Blue on stage in 2017 at the Zalgirio Arena in
Lithuania – copyright © Paul D. H. Baylay

Plate 16: 'Blue'

Bottom: Blue on stage during the Colours tour in 2015 –
copyright © Paul D. H. Baylay